WRITING FOR ENGINEERS

Palgrave Study Skills

Authoring a PhD
Business Degree Success
Career Skills
Critical Thinking Skills
e-Learning Skills (2nd edn)
Effective Communication for
  Arts and Humanities Students
Effective Communication for
  Science and Technology
The Exam Skills Handbook
The Foundations of Research
The Good Supervisor
How to Manage your Arts, Humanities and
  Social Science Degree
How to Manage your Distance and
  Open Learning Course
How to Manage your Postgraduate Course
How to Manage your Science and
  Technology Degree
How to Study Foreign Languages
How to Write Better Essays (2nd edn)
IT Skills for Successful Study
The International Student Handbook
Making Sense of Statistics
The Mature Student's Guide to Writing (2nd edn)
The Personal Tutor's Handbook
The Postgraduate Research Handbook (2nd edn)
Presentation Skills for Students
The Principles of Writing in Psychology

Professional Writing (2nd edn)
Researching Online
Research Using IT
Skills for Success
The Study Abroad Handbook
The Student's Guide to Writing (2nd edn)
The Student Life Handbook
The Study Skills Handbook (3rd edn)
Study Skills for International Postgraduates
Study Skills for Speakers of English as
  a Second Language
Studying the Built Environment
Studying Business at MBA and Masters Level
Studying Economics
Studying History (3rd edn)
Studying Law (2nd edn)
Studying Mathematics and its Applications
Studying Modern Drama (2nd edn)
Studying Physics
Studying Programming
Studying Psychology (2nd edn)
Teaching Study Skills and Supporting Learning
Work Placements – A Survival Guide for Students
Writing for Nursing and Midwifery Students
Write it Right
Writing for Engineers (3rd edn)

Palgrave Study Skills: Literature

General Editors: John Peck and Martin Coyle

How to Begin Studying English Literature
  (3rd edn)
How to Study a Jane Austen Novel (2nd edn)
How to Study a Charles Dickens Novel
How to Study Chaucer (2nd edn)
How to Study an E. M. Forster Novel
How to Study James Joyce
How to Study Linguistics (2nd edn)

How to Study Modern Poetry
How to Study a Novel (2nd edn)
How to Study a Poet
How to Study a Renaissance Play
How to Study Romantic Poetry (2nd edn)
How to Study a Shakespeare Play (2nd edn)
How to Study Television
Practical Criticism

Writing for Engineers

Third edition

Joan van Emden

palgrave
macmillan

First edition 1990
Reprinted four times
Second edition 1998
Reprinted four times
Third edition published 2005 by
PALGRAVE MACMILLAN
Houndmills, Basingstoke, Hampshire RG21 6XS and
175 Fifth Avenue, New York, N.Y. 10010
Companies and representatives throughout the world

PALGRAVE MACMILLAN is the global academic imprint of the Palgrave Macmillan division of St. Martin's Press, LLC and of Palgrave Macmillan Ltd. Macmillan® is a registered trademark in the United States, United Kingdom and other countries. Palgrave is a registered trademark in the European Union and other countries.

ISBN-13: 978-1-4039-4600-3
ISBN-10: 1-4039-4600-0

This book is printed on paper suitable for recycling and made from fully managed and sustained forest sources. Logging, pulping and manufacturing processes are expected to conform to the environmental regulations of the country of origin.

A catalogue record for this book is available from the British Library.

A catalog record for this book is available from the Library of Congress.

10   9   8   7
14   13   12   11   10   09   08

Printed and bound in Great Britain by CPD Wales, Blaina

To Marta and Richard
with my love

Contents

6 Writing for publication

7 The presentation of written information

Comments on and solutions to activities

Preface

Writing is probably that part of a working life which engineers, in company with many technical people, most dislike. Unfortunately, the more successful they are in their profession, the more time they will spend sitting at the computer preparing to convey technical information to colleagues, customers and clients.

Modern technology makes the chore of writing easier, but does not help engineers who want to present convincing arguments clearly and concisely. This book looks at the basic skills of spelling, punctuation and grammar, and also at appropriate style, conventional formats and the effective presentation of written information. Its aim is to give confidence to a wide range of engineers, undergraduates and research students, managers and consultants, indeed anyone who in the course of a working life needs help and encouragement in facing the challenge of writing well.

This challenge is as important and as daunting at the time of preparing a third edition as it was earlier. Technology has developed in ways that affect communication profoundly: in the second edition, email was viewed as an untried and limited way to transmit technical data. It is now perhaps the major means of communication, outstripping the fax and making the memo obsolete. These changes are reflected in this book. The second edition was widely used by members of the construction industries, and this too is reflected in the range of examples given and discussed.

In the third edition, as in the first and second, many of these examples are real life, taken from university work or company documentation. I continue to be grateful to all the hundreds of anonymous engineers whom I meet on technical writing courses, who have generously given me permission to use their writing and explained it to me. In particular, I should like to thank Dr J. B. Grimbleby and Dr A. J. Pretlove, both of the University of Reading, for their continuing help and support; similarly, I am indebted to Dr Martin Coutie and Dr Martyn Ramsden for permission to use some of their writing, Dr Ben Cosh, also of the University of Reading, and Jennifer Easteal for advice about the presentation of mathematical material, Dr Alex Kerr for his help and advice, and Anne Pinnock for help with the typescript. Any errors which remain are my own.

Joan van Emden

How to use this book

It's unlikely that you will want to sit down and read this book from beginning to end as if it were a novel. You are more likely to need to look up a *theme*, for instance how to prepare an article for publication, or a *type of difficulty*, for instance when to use a colon, or a *specific word confusion*, for instance the difference between principal and principle. You may also want to *check up on your own knowledge*, perhaps to find out whether or not you can punctuate accurately.

This book has been designed to help you to find the information you need as easily and quickly as possible. The **contents list** at the start includes a breakdown of each chapter, so that you can see the themes it covers. When you look at the individual chapter, you will see not only these topics but also where there are activities, so that if you want to check on your punctuation, you will see that there is an activity on the subject on page 54 of Chapter 3, with a suggested answer and often an appropriate comment at the end of the book.

The **index** at the end of the book will guide you to specific topics, so that you can look up 'colon' and you will be given a page reference and also a cross-reference to 'semi-colon', as the two are often confused.

There is also, at the end of the book, an **alphabetical sequence of words and phrases** that are discussed individually in the text. If, for instance, you are unsure of the difference between 'affect' and 'effect', you could look these words up in the list, and find a page reference which will guide you immediately to the section dealing with this confusion.

Finally, the book is full of helpful **examples**. Others are also to be found as the answers to the activities. There is, for instance, an example of a short report and covering letter on pages 133–5; these are presented as the suggested version of Activity 4.2 given on pages 70–1, but they may also be useful to you simply as examples to look at and think about.

1 Introduction

Reading maketh a full man; conference a ready man; and writing an exact man. (Sir Francis Bacon, *Essays,* 1597)

▶ Reading, discussing and writing

Communication as described by Sir Francis Bacon in the late sixteenth century is much the same as the communication of a practising engineer – man or woman – today. Reading, discussing and writing take up a large part of a working life, and through these activities knowledge is broadened, abilities are sharpened and reactions become more focused; the experience and expertise of the professional engineer are presented precisely and effectively.

This book is primarily concerned with the third aspect, writing, but the other two are equally important. Engineers must find out what is happening in their field, nationally and internationally; they must keep up to date with current practice and study the exact requirements of their companies and their clients. They must read the relevant documentation and be ready to respond to it if their knowledge is to be 'full', that is, sufficient to allow them to make appropriate decisions.

It would perhaps be brave, and certainly foolhardy, to take all such decisions in isolation. Bacon's second requirement, 'conference', involves engineers in meeting people, talking to their clients, giving instructions and making presentations, and discussing day-to-day problems with other engineers. Cooperation and mutual support result from such interaction, especially if 'conference' includes the underrated ability to listen well.

Writing, says Bacon, makes the writer 'exact'. In transforming ideas into written words, engineers have to make choices. They have to analyse exactly what is to be expressed, identify the readership, and decide on the appropriate format and style. In the education and training which made them engineers, they discovered the need for careful, precise and logical thought. In learning to be writers, they must apply the same criteria. Technical knowledge has to be communicated accurately, and as engineers write letters, outline their proposals, prepare specifications or plan reports, they must again be careful, precise and logical. They must have constantly in mind the needs of their readers, adjusting the amount of detail in the light of such needs and presenting the material in a logical form which can be identified easily and used with confidence.

▶ Confidence

Confidence is a key word in this book. Engineers, generally speaking, prefer to do the job rather than write about it. When faced with the blank computer screen, they have to start by making difficult decisions. Which words should they choose and in what order? What are the conventions they should follow? How can they hold the reader's attention? How can they write convincingly?

▶ Care, precision and logic are necessary to thinking and writing

Writing for Engineers provides guidance in the use of words, construction of sentences and organisation of paragraphs. It also looks at some of the most important types of format, both traditional such as the letter and more modern such as email, and discusses the conventions which should be followed. Most of all, this book aims to give engineering writers the confidence that they are conveying their information accurately and clearly. They are thus not only able to do the work, but also to write about it in a professional way.

Nevertheless, accuracy by itself is not enough to hold the attention of readers and convince them of the writer's point of view. Engineers have been known to go to extreme lengths in order to make an impact. One young professional, faced with the problem of presenting monthly reports which seemed to be regularly ignored, wrote one report in verse. His manager was, as you might expect, surprised. He called the young man into his office and held forth at length about this aberrant behaviour. When he paused to ask what the writer had to say for himself, he was even more surprised and, one hopes, abashed at the reply: 'This is the first time you've taken the trouble to discuss my report with me.'

Shock tactics apparently work, but are not recommended. If reports are written concisely, if the information is easily assimilated and the format well chosen, they will probably be read. What is certain is that if they are long-winded and unstructured, they will be ignored for as long as possible and finally read unhappily, if at all.

▶ Reader goodwill

▶ Good writing generates reader goodwill

The best advice for the prospective writer is, then, as follows:

- identify your readers
- know what they already know and what they need to know
- find out how much technical knowledge they are likely to have and what their involvement with the project is
- have full and accurate information at your disposal
- formulate your objectives (what you want to get out of this piece of writing)
- analyse your readers' likely objectives, as far as you can
- have confidence in yourself and your material
- write.

▶ Identify your readers and their objectives, and your own objectives, before beginning to write

▶ Getting started

A last word: don't feel that you have to begin at the beginning. The first sentence or paragraph is almost always the most difficult. Choose a simple, straightforward factual section which you feel comfortable with, and write it first. Then move to the next easiest section, and when you feel ready, move on. Your confidence will have received a boost, and by the time you reach the first section of your document (quite late in the writing process), you will have had considerable practice in the art of good writing. You are already 'exact'.

▶ Don't feel that you have to begin at the beginning

▶ Confidence grows with the practice of good writing

▶ Summary

- ▶ Care, precision and logic are necessary to thinking and writing
- ▶ Good writing generates reader goodwill
- ▶ Identify your readers and their objectives, and your own objectives, before beginning to write
- ▶ Don't feel that you have to begin at the beginning
- ▶ Confidence grows with the practice of good writing

2 Vocabulary

Some people like words and others like numbers. The sad truth is that those who like words rarely like numbers too and vice versa. Engineers often have love affairs with figures (having passed a range of mathematically oriented examinations in order to become engineers) but tend to feel that words are out to get them. As a result, they are uneasy about writing continuous prose and long for the release of a friendly equation.

▶ Choice of words

Words are indeed difficult in the English language. They are spelt in odd ways, often pronounced differently from the way they look, may sound the same as each other but have different meanings, and there are so many of them. It is a great advantage to have a language which is rich in synonyms (words which mean more or less the same thing), but there is a catch in this: which words should we choose?

The answer to this question is in four parts. We should choose words that are:

- understood by the reader
- familiar without being hackneyed
- accurate
- as simple as the subject matter allows.

The first of these points is sometimes overlooked. Engineers often write for a wide audience, not all of whom will have the same specialist knowledge. One of the early, preparatory questions to be asked before beginning to write any document is about the knowledge and experience levels of the intended readership. Will most of the readers understand the technical terms used? If not, and if help is not readily available, they will quickly become irritated with the writer and the text; they may even stop reading. There is of course a danger in overexplaining, seeming to patronise the readers; if too much is explained, they will soon be just as annoyed, and may stop reading. Readers often have different levels of expertise from those of the writer, but it is the writer's job to decide how much explanation is appropriate, and then to be consistent.

The best way out of the difficulty in most cases is to include a glossary of technical terms and abbreviations which might be unknown to at least some readers. Such glossaries are common in reports and specifications, and are helpful to those who need them. As long as the existence of the glossary is made clear in the contents list, readers can look up what they don't know. At the same time, a glossary is unobtrusive for those who have the appropriate specialist knowledge; they can simply ignore it. In the case of a shorter document such as a letter or email, it is usually better simply to write the terms in full or add a short explanatory phrase rather than risk leaving the recipient bewildered.

▶ English is an international language

The readership for some technical writing, however, will be much wider; an engineer may be writing for an international readership. On the whole, technical terms will cause less difficulty than the 'simple' words in between – worldwide, many engineers receive their technical training in

English. It is words or expressions which are used by native English speakers in a colloquial way, or which refer to concepts local to western European culture which cause the greatest difficulty. 'Letting off steam' might sound to someone unfamiliar with the expression as if it applied to an old-fashioned railway engine rather than an engineer under stress, while a 'bank holiday' might suggest a day on which banks enjoyed their own day of rest rather than a national holiday (see also p. 117 for the implications of this problem when writing for publication).

The same principles apply to engineering writing for a readership which is not primarily English speaking. Expressions which are 'local' should be avoided, and the writer should show sensitivity, as far as possible, in not using expressions which are unnecessarily complicated; for example, 'on no account do this' can be expressed more simply and clearly as 'do not do this'. Nevertheless, if the only accurate word or expression is rare or complex, it must be used, as accuracy cannot be sacrificed to familiarity. In such cases, a note might be appropriate, or, better still, a diagram. Illustrations are on the whole more easily and widely understood than paragraphs of explanation. Writers should always be aware of their readers, remembering that engineering information is sometimes translated into other languages; there is no point in making life harder than necessary for the translators.

▶ Use words and expressions which readers understand; if appropriate, include a glossary

▶ American English

Many engineers work for American or multinational companies, and it is worth remembering that we often fail to share our common language. Differences in spelling are well known: color, traveling, center are all acceptable in American English, and as a result may be the forms desired by the computer's dictionary. It is always worth setting the spellcheck for the type of English used, that is, English rather than American English. When meanings are different, the problem is more serious. A UK gallon is about a sixth more than a US gallon, an English chemist is an American druggist, although in both countries the word 'chemist' is used for a scientist whose specialism is chemistry. A billion is now standardised at 1000 million on both sides of the Atlantic, but the British ground floor (American first floor) may still cause misunderstanding, and 'to table a motion' at an American meeting is to set it aside – exactly the opposite to the British meaning. The only guideline is that if you find yourself arguing with an American colleague, check that it is not the language which is dividing you rather than the subject of debate. If you frequently exchange written material, keep an American dictionary next to the English one.

▶ Foreign words and phrases

English itself has assimilated a great number of foreign words and phrases; it also uses some which have not been assimilated but remain 'foreign' and are often put into italics as a result. In the past, professional writing was full of these expressions, especially in letters (the 5th ult., viz.) and published references (op. cit., ibid.). Many people nowadays do not understand such expressions, which are seen as pompous, 'showing off'. Unless there is a good reason for using a foreign expression, or it is widely accepted, avoid it. If you need to use it, decide whether it has become part of the English language or still needs italics, and then be consistent in its use.

▶ Prefixes

Prefixes (additions to the beginnings of words), however, often have their origins in foreign languages, and it is useful to be able to recognise them. Bi means two or twice (originally Latin), and knowing that, we can more easily understand words like bilateral, bipartite or binary. Some prefixes are easily confused, such as ante (before) and anti (against), hyper (beyond, above), hypo (under, below), inter (between) and intro (inside).

Activity 2.1 Prefixes

Decide what the prefix means in each of the following words, and find other words which also use these prefixes.

Ambivalent, homogenous, malfunction, metabolism, retrograde

▶ Accuracy

In technical writing, words must be used accurately and the reader must understand the way in which they are used. Accuracy has three aspects:

- words must be used so that the intended meaning is conveyed precisely
- the words which appear in the text must be the exact words that the author intended
- the reader must recognise the words as appropriate in their context.

All these criteria present problems.

Inaccurate use of words is usually the result of imprecise thinking. The engineer who produced the following example did not consider exactly what needed to be said before putting fingers to keyboard:

> The purpose of this email is to notify all company personnel involved with the Zero project of the present situation regarding outstanding items not delivered to the customer yet for one reason or another.

As a result of this failure to identify the message, the writer uses unnecessary and confusing words. 'The purpose of this email is to notify' is self-evident. Items which have not been delivered to the customer yet *are* outstanding items. The sentence peters out with the strange comment 'for one reason or another'. This sounds worrying – all sorts of things are going wrong – but it means nothing. Words are used so loosely that the recipients must have felt as if they were holding tightly onto jelly, which oozed through their fingers.

The writer needs to clarify the message first of all:

> We've problems of late delivery on the Zero project. This is the current situation.

The chosen method of communication is an email. The subject line can be 'Zero project: late delivery' and the email will of course be sent to the appropriate people, and so they don't have to be told who they are. All that is needed is a brief sentence or two about the present situation and a suitable signing off (see p. 62 for discussion of email format).

Illogicality in writing can result from similar poor planning. Words convey the wrong meaning, for example:

> As the metal becomes harder and hence an increase in carbon content, the metal tends not to increase its reduction, but instead the area is less than a metal with less carbon.

The underlying mistake in this sentence is perhaps the writer's ignorance of the measurement 'reduction of area', that is, the ductility of the metal. While there has been an attempt to relate hardness to carbon content, the message has not been thought through. The hardness of the metal does not, as is suggested, result ('hence') in an increase in carbon content; rather, as the carbon content increases, we find an increase in hardness. The word 'hence' is totally misleading. The oddly expressed 'tends not to increase its reduction' is confusing, not least because of the juxtaposition of 'not' with 'increase' and 'reduction'. The last part of the sentence is probably an attempt to reiterate the first part, but the writer is too ill at ease with the information to be able to say anything on the subject clearly. The sentence might be written simply as:

> As the carbon content increases, so does the hardness, and at the same time the ductility of the metal is reduced.

▶ Identify the message and plan its expression

▶ Pairs of words

Words discussed in this section
Stationery and stationary, draft and draught, cite, sight and site, moral and morale, personal and personnel, accede and exceed, access and assess, principle and principal, affect and effect, advice and advise, device and devise, practice and practise, licence and license, disinterested and uninterested, complex and complicated, imply and infer, deny and refute, expect and anticipate

English contains many words which sound alike but have different spellings and different meanings. A writer in a hurry can easily confuse words which, under other circumstances, would easily be distinguished. Such words are *stationery* (writing paper) and *stationary* (without movement), *principal* (chief) and *principle* (underlying rule or moral basis), *draft* (rough version) and *draught* (current of air). Sometimes a group of three words can cause confusion, such as *cite* (quote), *sight* (vision) and *site* (area of land). The spellcheck is no help in drawing attention to a misuse of these words, and perhaps as a result, such mistakes are surprisingly common. The result can be faintly comical, as in the case of the student who wrote:

> Diamond is tough and is covalent, but other chain polymers may be extremely week.

Some pairs of words sound almost, but not quite, the same and are easily confused, such as *moral* (ethical) and *morale* (emotional condition) or *personal* (belonging to the individual) and *personnel* (staff). Some such difficulties arise regularly in engineering writing, for instance *accede* and *exceed*; *access* and *assess*; *principle* and *principal*:

accede=assent to ('he acceded to my request')

exceed=surpass ('he exceeded the speed limit')

access=entry ('access to the building')

assess=weigh up ('assess the capability of the machine')

principle=moral principle ('his principles prevented his cheating')

principal=main, chief ('the principal reason for the change . . .')

A further common example is slightly more complicated: *affect* and *effect*. The difficulty arises because 'effect' can be both noun and verb, and also because many people do not pronounce the words clearly, probably because they are not sure which is which! *Affect* is a verb, which means 'to have an influence on', as in:

Studying engineering to an advanced level has affected his job prospects.

Effect can be a verb, meaning 'to bring about', as in:

Study, hard work and experience combined to effect an improvement in his career prospects.

Effect can also be a noun, meaning 'an influence' or 'the result', for example:

His overseas experience has had an effect on his career pattern.

The effect of his hard work has been rapid promotion.

Other pairs of words which often give trouble are those which depend for their spelling on the way in which they are used. Some have a useful difference in pronunciation, such as: *advice/advise* and *device/devise*, while others sound the same, such as: *practice/practise* and *licence/license*. In each case, the noun has a *c* and the verb has an *s*. For example:

I can advise you to study engineering, but will you take my advice?

He perfected a device for sounding the alarm but could not devise a way of ensuring that people would respond.

Sometimes words with a similar derivation have nowadays moved further apart so that their meanings are different:

- *disinterested*=impartial, without prejudice
- *uninterested*=having no interest in (almost bored)

- *complex* = involved, technically difficult

- *complicated* = mixed up, difficult to untangle

Other words which are often confused are:

imply and *infer*	*imply* = suggest, hint
	infer = understand, assume a meaning
deny and *refute*	*deny* = simply to declare that something is not true
	refute = to prove that something is not true
expect and anticipate	*expect* = to think that something will happen in the future
	anticipate = to take action in the light of that expectation

I implied that she might soon be promoted, and she inferred that a senior position was becoming vacant.

The accused denied that he had been at the scene of the crime, but was unable to produce evidence to refute the charge.

Any engineer would have expected a problem with such a delicate machine, but Jim had anticipated it by bringing a backup.

In all these cases, the problems are obvious but the solutions much less so. A writer of technical information must be aware of words and the ways in which they can be confused, alert to the look and sound of words, and careful and attentive in both listening and writing. Pronunciation can have a direct impact on spelling: a mistake such as 'failiure' is the result of saying the extra 'i' after the 'l' and then hearing and writing it (to be fair, the spell-check would pick this up); 'presence' and 'presents' can sound exactly the same if they are carelessly spoken; the misspelling 'maintainance' is usually the effect of pronouncing the word that way rather than, correctly, 'maintenance'. As with most problems of English, critical reading will help, together with a determination to make friends with words as well as numbers.

▶ Choose words with care; read critically

Activity 2.2 Word confusion

Identify the mistakes in the following passage.

The stationery vehicle was the principle cause of the traffic jam. Motorists were advised to find a different route until the police could affect a solution to the problem. Later, some inferred that the authorities had been disinterested until the chief constable's car had been delayed, all charge that was strenuously refuted in their statement but was sighted next day in the papers.

▶ Synonyms

Earlier in this chapter, the comment was made that English is particularly rich in synonyms – words which have exactly the same, or sometimes a very slightly different, meaning. However, apart from the dictionary definition, there is also the feel of a word; we know almost instinctively which word to choose for a particular context. *Difficult, hard* and *troublesome* can all mean the same thing, yet we would not be likely to describe a difficult question as troublesome or a troublesome toothache as difficult.

Some synonyms cause particular problems because, while their meanings are the same, the implications are different. A *request* is different from a *desire to know* or a *demand to know*; the speaker might prefer to be thought of as *forceful*, while listeners might use the word *aggressive*. It depends on the point of view! We choose words not only for their meaning but also for their implications: so we may congratulate a friend for showing *determination* while deprecating the *stubbornness* of an opponent. We may hesitate to *recommend* a course of action, and so we *suggest* it, which sounds milder, and of course if things go wrong, we can always claim that it was 'only a suggestion'.

▶ Precision

Words discussed in this section
Power, aggravate, unique, former and latter, number, majority and fewer, amount, greater (lesser) and less, regular, where and when

Dictionaries can be dangerous. They are rarely capable of showing such fine shades of meaning, and we have to be sensitive to the impact of the words we choose. Words also change their meaning according to their context. If we look up *power* in the dictionary, we find a wide range of meanings, including *ability to act, vigour, energy, government, personal ascendancy, authorisation, influential person, magnifying capacity* and so on. The writer must be sure that the intended meaning is clear to the reader. We know what we mean if we talk about 'six to the power of ten' or 'switching on the power supply' or 'the power of the pianist's interpretation of a concerto', but if we say that we have the *'power'* to make a particular piece of information known, do we mean the *'authority'* or just the *'ability'*? Our reader might not be sure which is the correct interpretation, and we must clarify our intention.

Casual speech sometimes misuses words in a way which is not acceptable in the written language. *Aggravate* means 'to make worse' (not 'to annoy'). *Unique* means that there is only one example in existence, not that it is rare. *Former* and *latter* are the first and second of two, never more than two; the correct use is shown in the following example:

> The lights and the steering need to be adjusted: the former can be done at once but the latter will take us a bit longer and so we will need the car tomorrow as well as today.

Other groups of words are often misused: *number, majority* and *fewer* always refer to several objects or people, while *amount, greater* (or *lesser*) *part* and *less* refer to only one object or person. For example:

> There was a large number of delegates, and the majority favoured the new agreement. Fewer than a hundred objected.
> There was a large amount of work still to be done, the greater part of which, on this occasion, had to be completed during the night. Fewer workers and less time will be needed in future.

Accuracy of expression also means that the words chosen are in themselves precise. Words and phrases such as *fairly, quite, rather, to a limited extent* and *in due course* produce a vague, hesitant impression, while *very, extremely, mainly* and *substantially* sound important but convey no precise picture, for example:

> Our experiments were fairly successful and we are generally hopeful that we shall be able to make the results public in due course.

This means very little. What is 'fairly successful'? Some of the experiments, or on some occasions? What percentages? 'Generally hopeful'? All of them or only most of them? Most of the time? When they aren't feeling depressed? 'In due course'? Next week? Next year? Eventually, if we're lucky? While it would be wrong to suggest that such words and phrases are always unhelpful and should therefore never be used, they can be irritating to the reader who is looking for precise information. If it is possible to be exact, then be exact:

> We were successful with 60% of our experiments, and provided there are no unforeseen problems, we shall make the results public within the next two months.

So now they know!

Engineering information must always be accurate; it must also be conveyed accurately. Lack of precision in, for example, a specification or a report can have serious implications, and it is often the case that while the technical terms are correctly used, the small English words which appear in between the technical words cause ambiguity or misunderstanding. Two short examples illustrate this:

> In future, the company will need less skilled workers for the night shift.
> In future, the company will need fewer skilled workers for the night shift.

Which meaning was intended? In the first sentence, the same number of workers could have less training or experience and so less skill; in the second, the company will not need so many workers, perhaps because they are highly skilled. There is clearly a significant difference. *Less* describes the degree of skill, while *fewer* refers to the number of workers.

A similar problem arises, again because of the imprecise use of words, in the following example:

> Maintenance shall be carried out at regular intervals or where there is evidence of malfunction.

'At regular intervals' means little more than 'in due course'; how regular is regular? Every ten years? 'Or' does not really signify an alternative, but an additional reason for maintenance. 'Where' is not used in its usual meaning of 'the place where'; in casual conversation, we often confuse 'where' and 'when' and little harm is done; in the above sentence, the difference between place and time is crucial. This might be rephased as:

> Maintenance shall be carried out at six-monthly intervals and whenever there is evidence of malfunction.

As we can see from these examples, words which seem in themselves to be unimportant can change the meaning for the reader.

Words must not only be used accurately, they must also appear accurately in the text. This means that they are spelt correctly and the printed version says exactly what the writer intended. Checking, an important stage in the production of any document, is discussed later (see p. 120). It is enough at this stage to point out that unchecked work can look very odd on the page, as in the case of the engineer who wrote, in awful handwriting, '50ft', and was appalled to discover that it had been reproduced (unchecked) as 'soft'.

▶ Spelling new words

Spelling is a nightmare to many engineers, slightly mitigated nowadays by the computer spellcheck facility. As we have seen, this has great advantages but also limitations, and it is still worth having a dictionary on the desk. Some words will in any case escape because they are too new or too technical for either aid. It is worth adding such words, if they will be used frequently, to the computer dictionary, but with the reservation that the spelling should be checked first. It is not unknown for words to be added incorrectly, causing continuing problems.

Both management and modern technology produce new words or reuse old words in a new form. Some have limited application, while others become widely known and used. For example, people in the past would have registered 'mouse' as a small furry animal; most people now would just as quickly think of it as a device for selecting objects or defining positions on the screen. Sometimes modern developments give rise to complicated-sounding expressions, such as 'negative corporate worth', defined as the disadvantage for a subsidiary company of belonging to a larger corporation. Technology seems to favour composite words made up of words which in themselves are short and simple: 'workstation' and 'spreadsheet' are two examples. On the whole, such words are joined up without a hyphen, although they can become top-heavy, as can too many words containing hyphens (for further comment on the use of hyphens, see p. 51). It is not easy to read a sentence like the following:

> This is network-transparent, operating-system-independentand portable... it promises to revolutionise high-end computing.

If the writer is in doubt about how to write new words, the best guidance is probably to check what the major journals in the field are doing. The engineering institutions are likely to face such questions early on, and their decisions may well set the standard for future usage.

Since English is a living language, usage that was once 'wrong' may gradually have become acceptable. The most common example of this is 'data', a plural word (singular datum) nowadays generally used as a singular, the rationale for this being that data is a collective noun like 'group' or 'committee'. However, such developments, at least in the short term, do not influence similar words, and 'strata' and 'criteria' are still considered to be plural (singulars stratum, criterion).

▶ Common spelling problems

Old words can be just as worrying as new words, and there are many common words in English that are just difficult to spell. There is little logic about English spelling, and the rules that exist generally have a great many exceptions. The only one which is worth remembering is 'i before e except after c, as long as the sound is ee'; this rule (provided it is remembered in its entirety) is actually helpful, as there are many instances in which it is followed (believe, receive, height) and comparatively few exceptions (seize). It is always worth making up mnemonics for one's personal list of most hated words; the more silly the idea, the easier it is to remember it (for instance, 'liaison' needs more than one person and so contains two i's).

A common confusion is between 'there', 'their' and 'they're'. An easy way to remember the first two is to think of 'there' as 't-here'; 'here' refers to place, and so does 'there'; 'their' means 'belonging to them', which has no 'place' element, that is, no 'here' in it. The third, 'they're', means 'they are', and such an abbreviation will rarely be used in technical writing (see p. 91 for formality of style).

▶ Use the computer's spellcheck and a dictionary, both with great care!

▶ Simple language

Words should be as simple as the context allows. Some writers seem to aim at confusion, as, for instance, does the author of the following guideline for the numbering of tables in reports:

Tables will be given successive decimal integer numbers of ascending value starting at unity.

This means no more than:

Number tables sequentially from 1.

Indeed, 'from 1' would almost certainly be assumed by the reader and could be left out. Fourteen words have been reduced to three! Yet the real-life sentence quoted above in its original form is typical of much engineering writing. Instead of making their point in a simple, straightforward way, writers wrap their message in long sentences made up of words which are intended to sound impressive. It is amazing what peculiarities can result. A recent development is to use nouns as verbs, 'task', usually a noun, being a good example: someone was described as being 'tasked with a mission'; the most interesting feature of this expression is that noun and verb could be exchanged, he could have been 'missioned with a task'. He was, in fact, given a job.

There seem to be various reasons for such pompous and wordy language. One is undoubtedly the need to hide unpleasant or embarrassing information, as in the following example:

Following our recent meeting, we feel we must put in writing which we believe to be the justifying factors leading to our proposed modest increases in costs.

Clearly, the writer is uncomfortable. Whatever should have been put in writing has actually been left out ('the factors' or some such expression), and the unfortunate word 'modest' has been dragged in to make the writer feel better. Modest by whose standards? Why should the company concerned stress that the rise was 'justified'? What have the writer's feelings and beliefs got to do with the situation? The use of 'recent' suggests the subtext 'I should have done this sooner and am embarrassed to give the date'. It would have been better to come straight to the point:

In the light of our meeting on 21 January, I confirm that we shall shortly raise our prices.

If it is really necessary to say why this has happened, a short sentence of explanation could follow.

Pompous words are also used because they are felt to be more influential than everyday words. Writers 'acquaint their readers with' or 'advise their readers of', rather than simply telling or informing them. They 'render assistance' rather than 'give help' and they 'subject to examination' rather than 'examine'. They 'are in a position to undertake' rather than 'can' or 'are able to', and they 'peruse' documents when most people would read them; they prefer to 'utilise' rather than to 'use'. In so doing, they waste everybody's time and irritate the reader; they do not impress. Such inflated language, full of self-importance, may disguise the information. The engineer who wrote:

> The number of samples tested is important. If it is too small, poor results can be concealed or indicate erroneous behavioural characteristics.

failed to analyse what was written. If the sample is too small, results give false indications, that is, give poor results. The sentence goes in a circle. The meaning behind all this was probably the obvious fact that:

> A sufficient number of samples must be tested before the result can be considered valid.

▶ Use simple words as far as the context permits

▶ Avoiding clichés and slang

The final criterion in the choice of words is that they should be familiar to the reader without being hackneyed. One of the problems of the pompous words discussed above is that they are also rare and therefore not easily understood. We have been brought up with a certain amount of 'official-speak' from public organisations, such as 'tender the correct fare' or 'passengers alight here', which are recognisable, but not natural. Few of us would use 'tender' or 'alight' in other contexts. Writers should use words which readers can recognise and feel at home with.

However, it is possible to go too far the other way. Expressions which are overused become clichés, dull and lifeless phrases which have ceased to make any impact. 'At the end of the day', meaning 'finally' or 'eventually'; 'at this present moment in time', meaning 'now'; 'leave no stone unturned', meaning 'try hard' are all such expressions, used to the point at which they distract or irritate the reader and so undermine confidence in the information itself.

Slang belongs only to the spoken word and then only in casual conversation between friends. In writing, it jars on the reader and interrupts concentration. There is an example of this effect on page 43, in the passage beginning 'It should be noted...'. The writer used the (in this context) pompous word 'terminate' and then the slang expression 'start again from scratch'. The transition is unpleasant, as the reader is jerked from over-formal language into everyday speech. Slang has no place in engineering writing.

▶ Clichés and slang distract the reader and should be avoided

▶ Jargon

Jargon, however, comes in two kinds, one acceptable and the other not. The former is professional, understood by other engineers in the same discipline, but not part of the everyday language of the non-specialist. It would be impossible to manage without this sort of jargon, as it allows an expert to communicate easily with other experts. Both writers and readers take for granted a range of such expressions, assuming mutual understanding. Examples of such jargon in the field of expert systems are 'antecedent', 'backward chaining', 'blind search', 'control structure' and 'declarative knowledge representation'. Two possible dangers arise from the use of such terms. One is that the reader will not understand, and the engineering writer must always be alert to the need for acceptable communication with the 'outside world', for instance with clients who have less specialist knowledge than the writer.

The other danger is more insidious: both writer and reader may assume understanding when none exists. For example, in the list given above, 'antecedent' means the left-hand side of a production rule, that is, the pattern needed to make the rule applicable. The dictionary definition of antecedent is 'preceding circumstance' or, in logic, 'the part of a conditional proposition on which the other depends'. We can see a relationship between the expert system definition and the lay definition, but they are not interchangeable. Expert jargon must be used with care.

The other kind of jargon is widespread and horrible. It uses words unnecessarily, sounds pompous and either lacks or conceals meaning. There are temporarily popular words and phrases such as 'function' ('the engineering function' is the job of the engineer, that is, engineering), 'facility' (as in 'the manufacturing facility' meaning the factory), and 'situation', which may be added to almost anything – a crisis situation, a late delivery situation, an overmanning situation. It doesn't mean anything. Such terms can be used effectively to disguise meaning, as in:

> The interactive function of the project manager with the team was such that it necessitated urgent implementation of the staff transfer policy.

In other words, the project manager could not get on with the team and someone had to be moved, fast. There are even buzz-word jargon generators (a nice piece of jargon in itself) which allow expressions to be put together in any order so that they form impressive but meaningless sentences:

A constant flow of effective information will maximise the probability of project success and minimise the cost and time required for standardisation of anticipated documentation.

If this means anything, it means 'let's get the communication right!'

▶ Professional jargon must be shared with the reader

▶ 'Popular' jargon and slang should be avoided

Activity 2.3 Inaccurate writing

Rewrite the following sentence accurately, in a shorter and clearer form.

Members of the team made an attempt to initiate the process, but couldn't percieve how to get their act together. The position was aggravated by an amount of software problems for which they were unable to device solutions. They were told to try again with less people involved and at the end of the day were able to produce a more advantageous result which avoided the crisis situation that had been anticipated.

▶ Summary

▶ Use words and expressions which readers understand; if necessary, give a glossary
▶ Identify the message and plan its expression
▶ Choose words with care; read critically
▶ Use the computer's spellcheck and a dictionary, both with great care!
▶ Use simple words as far as the context permits
▶ Clichés and slang distract the reader and should be avoided
▶ Professional jargon must be shared with the reader
▶ Popular jargon and slang should be avoided

3 Sentences and punctuation

A sentence is as long as a piece of Sellotape and, for some people, more sticky. This is a useful analogy, as it avoids the cliché ('as long as a piece of string') and at the same time gives positively helpful information. Sellotape is an excellent product, provided that *the length of tape is right for its purpose*. Too short a piece, and the paper fails to fasten the parcel; too long a piece, and tape, paper and fingers stick together in a nasty mess. Sentences are much the same. A very short sentence may fail to give the required information, or it may leave out essential elements such as a verb. A very long sentence often confuses itself, its writer and its reader, and ends up as a nasty mess. Sentences must be the right length for their purpose. Before looking more closely at sentence length and construction, we should say what a sentence is.

▶ Definition of a sentence

- A sentence is a group of words which makes sense in itself
- A sentence contains at least one main item of information to which various subsidiary ideas may be attached
- A sentence must contain at least one complete verb

The first aspect of this definition is most important, and many mistakes would be avoided if the writer asked, 'Does this make sense?' If it does not, it is not a sentence. Complete understanding may depend on knowledge of the context, but each sentence in itself should be intelligible to the reader. The beginnings of letters produce many mistakes of this kind:

In reply to your enquiry about maintenance.
With reference to your telephone call.

These are incomplete parts of sentences ('in reply to your enquiry' . . . what?) and do not make sense by themselves. What is more, they do not contain verbs. They are not sentences.

▶ Sentence composition and structure

A sentence should contain one or two items of information and not twenty-three. Engineers often feel unable to stop writing, and add sentence to sentence, separating sentences by commas, until they have moved far away from the first piece of information, as in the following example:

> At every stage when an error creeps in, an operator interrupts and corrects the problem, when really the system should be set up either to prevent the error occurring in the first place, or to be able to detect the error and correct the problem automatically.

There are two pieces of information here: what happens at present, and what is desirable. This immediately suggests two sentences:

> At present, errors have to be corrected manually. The system should either prevent errors or, if this is not possible, detect and correct them automatically.

In this version, the number of words has been almost halved (25 instead of 46), and the meaning has been clarified, with a neat contrast between 'manually' and 'automatically'. Unnecessary words such as 'at every stage' and 'really' have been left out, and the two sentences are much better style than the clumsy version in one sentence.

There are two kinds of unit that can make up a sentence: **clauses**, which contain a verb, and **phrases**, which don't. In every sentence, the essential element is called the **main clause**: this may be just one word long, as in 'Stop!' which is acceptable as the single word is itself a verb. Usually there are several words in the main clause, as in:

> The car refused to start.

This main clause makes good sense, contains one main idea and has a complete verb, 'refused'. (We may question the word 'refused', on the grounds that the car had little choice in the matter, but the expression is widely used and so, perhaps, acceptable.) In other words, the main clause and the sentence are one and the same thing. However, such a sentence can be extended, for instance by a phrase, a group of words which do not contain a verb:

> On a cold, damp morning, the car refused to start.

We still have the main clause with its verb, but there is now additional information in the form of the phrase 'on a cold, damp morning'. It is worth noting that the phrase could occur in the middle of the main clause without affecting the structure of the sentence, as in:

> The car, on a cold, damp morning, refused to start.

In this type of construction, the intervening phrase is usually separated from the rest of the sentence by a pair of commas, as in the example. A phrase may be placed at any point of the sentence, even at the end:

> The car refused to start, on a cold, damp morning.

The reader will probably have noticed that there is a slight shift of emphasis: when the phrase comes in the middle of the sentence, it has more stress than at the end; in the earlier example, the weather is particularly worthy of comment, while the problem of the car is stressed more heavily if the description of the weather is placed later.

Phrases are often, although not always, descriptive of time or place: examples are 'in the afternoon', 'after working hours', 'at the same time', 'at the company's headquarters' and so on. They add to the meaning of the rest of the sentence, but as they do not contain a verb, they can never stand alone.

A sentence, then, will have a main clause and may contain one or more phrases. It may also have other clauses, **subordinate clauses**, which include verbs but which cannot, unlike the main clause, stand alone. These clauses expand the meaning of the main clause, often explaining how or why the main action was taken. For example, the writer may want to explain why the car refused to start, and therefore adds the subordinate clause 'because the battery was flat'. There may be some resentment about the inconvenient timing of the incident, and the writer adds another subordinate clause, 'when I was already late for work'. The sentence now reads as follows:

> On a cold, damp morning when I was already late for work, the car refused to start because the battery was flat.

This sentence is still acceptable, because all the information is linked to the original idea, but the reader may well feel that the limit for easy reading is near. Trouble arises if more ideas are added:

> On a cold, damp morning when I was already late for work, the car refused to start because the battery was flat, but my neighbour, who saw the problem, came out with jump leads, and both of us together started the car and I got to work only ten minutes late.

If we analyse this sentence, we find that it contains four main ideas:

1. the car refused to start
2. my neighbour came out with the jump leads
3. we started the car
4. I got to work

Each of these ideas has its subsidiary information:

1. on a cold, damp morning (phrase)
2. when I was already late for work (subsidiary clause)
3. my neighbour (phrase)
4. who saw the problem (subsidiary clause)
5. both of us together (phrase)
6. only ten minutes late (phrase)

None of these items by itself is a sentence (none makes sense by itself), but if each is added to the appropriate main idea (main clause, the one in bold italic type in each case), a sequence of good, readable sentences results:

1. On a cold, damp morning when I was already late for work, ***the car refused to start***.
2. ***My neighbour***, who saw the problem, ***came out with jump leads***.
3. Together, ***we started the car***.
4. ***I got to work*** only ten minutes late.

Each sentence now fulfils the criteria given in the definition, and we have a structured piece of writing, with all the events in the correct logical order.

▶ Simple and compound sentences

One more aspect of sentence structure is worth mentioning at this point. As we have seen, a sentence may have one major idea, in which case it is called a **simple sentence**. It is also possible for a sentence to have two or more major ideas of equal importance (a **compound sentence**), although the writer must take care not to get carried away by this possibility. The ideas must be closely linked and none must involve many words, or the sentence will become too long. The essential element of such a sentence is that there are words which make the connections – the ideas must not simply be placed one after the other with a comma in between, which is a common mistake in technical writing. The two words which most frequently act in this way are 'and' and 'but'; in each case they join together main clauses which could stand independently. Such joining words are known as **conjunctions**.

As an example, we might well decide, for reasons of style, to join together sentences 3 and 4 of the example given above:

Together, we started the car and I got to work only ten minutes late.

If we do so, then we have made a *decision* on the grounds of good style; we have not simply allowed the sentence to happen.

Understanding the basic structure of a sentence is an important stage in developing a good style. It gives the writer considerable power, both to show a clear logical sequence of events and stress specific ideas. The reader perceives that the writer is in command of the information and has presented it in a structured way. The reading is as easy as the content allows, provided that the sentences so constructed have not been allowed to grow out of control.

▶ Sentence length

A sentence, especially if it contains technical information, should not be so long that the reader is unable to assimilate the ideas. An average of 17–20 words is reasonable, with a maximum of about 40 words. Even if a sentence is correctly constructed, it will be difficult to untangle if it contains too many ideas (the 'Sellotape effect'), as we can see from the following example:

> Further to our recent meeting regarding electricity supply and utilisation, I would like very much to arrange a further meeting with you to discuss the subject, coupled with a general discussion on electrical applications and equipment capable of providing possible reductions in unit production costs, such as electric/steam generators and convection/radiant ovens coupled to load control equipment.

This amazing sentence contains 59 words and several ideas. Underneath it all is one simple unit (the main clause which is itself a complete sentence):

> I should like to arrange a further meeting.

Two subordinate ideas are added to the beginning of this:

1. further to our recent meeting
2. regarding electricity supply and utilisation

and one subordinate idea is added to the end:

3. to discuss the subject

This is quite enough for one sentence. However, our engineer sweeps on to the next basic idea:

> We could have a general discussion.

To this, yet another subordinate idea has been added:

1. about electrical applications and equipment

and, to make matters worse, further details follow:

2. capable of providing possible reductions in unit production costs

Refusing to give up, the writer moves into examples:

3. such as electric/steam generators and convection/radiant ovens coupled to load control equipment

The sentence is now a long way from the meeting which was to be arranged, and the reader is thoroughly confused. There are three main ideas in this monstrous sentence:

1. I should like to arrange a further meeting.
2. At the same time, we could discuss equipment.
3. I can give you examples of the kind of equipment I have in mind.

Subordinate ideas can now be grouped round each of these main ideas to form three sentences. In organising the information in this way, the writer might well decide that the second and third sentences belong in a new paragraph (see Chapter 4), and leave out redundant material such as 'to discuss the subject'; the pompous word 'utilisation' may be replaced by the simpler 'use'. The details could then be reorganised to produce a more logical and readable version:

> I should like to arrange a further meeting with you to continue our discussions of [date] on electricity supply and use.
> At the same time, we could have a general look at electrical applications and equipment [which are] capable of providing reductions in unit production costs. I have in mind electric/steam generators and convection/radiant ovens coupled to load control equipment.

Sometimes, as we have seen, a sentence contains only one basic idea; other sentences contain more than one basic idea, but the guidelines for sentence length always apply.

▶ Sentences contain one idea, or two or three closely related ideas which must be correctly joined together

In passing, it is worth noting that 'however' is not a conjunction, although it is often wrongly used as one. It either comments on the information:

> The initial cost of the machine is high. Maintenance, however, is relatively inexpensive.

or it is the equivalent of 'in whatever way':

> However we look at the problem, there is no easy solution.

We read these two sentences in different ways because of the punctuation (the two commas) in the former, and the absence of punctuation in the latter (see also p. 46).

Good style includes variety of sentence length. A few short sentences are direct and sometimes dramatic in their impact, as, for instance, the seven-word sentence which begins this paragraph. Too many short sentences, however, give a rather childish effect, as if the writer thinks that the reader will have difficulty with more complex sentences. It is better to look for logical connections between some of the sentences and join them in an appropriate way.

Perhaps the most important rule for good technical writing is to avoid overlong and overcomplicated sentences. Many other problems, especially those connected with punctuation and grammar, will disappear if sentence length is controlled. A sentence of more than about 40 words causes two areas of difficulty:

- *for the writer*, who finds it hard to organise the construction of the sentence if there are too many ideas to communicate at once
- *for the reader*, who finds it hard to assimilate the information in a long sentence, however well it is written.

The following sentence is not easy to read; it makes no concession to the reader:

> Due to the large inefficiency of resistor ballast drives, chopper drives have to be used for higher power applications in spite of the problems of being more complex, generating audible noise at the chopping frequency and possible interference, also iron losses in the motor.

We can analyse the problems as follows:

1. The sentence is too long, and contains too much information. It must be divided up.

2. The beginning 'due to' is poor style: it is ugly in itself and suggests that the information has been badly structured.
3. 'large inefficiency' is a strange expression, 'large' being generally associated with physical size rather than the scale of an abstract idea.
4. The most important information, 'chopper drives have to be used for higher power applications' receives little emphasis, especially as it follows a long and cumbersome introductory expression.
5. 'in spite of the problems of being' is both wordy and unnecessary, as what follows clearly are problems.
6. The four problems given are in two categories, inevitable and possible. 'Complexity' and 'noise' appear to be inevitable, while 'interference' is given as possible. There is then the apparent afterthought, 'iron losses in the motor', tacked on to the rest by a comma and 'also' – a clumsy and ungrammatical extension to the sentence. As this follows the 'possible' interference, the reader can assume that the iron losses are also possible rather than inevitable, although this is not made clear.

The passage can now be rewritten in a more acceptable form:

> For higher power applications, chopper drives must be used because resistor ballast drives are highly inefficient. Chopper drives, however, are complex, generate audible noise at the chopping frequency, and possibly cause interference and iron losses in the motor.

The need for chopper drives is now stated clearly in the first sentence. In the second, the problems of their use are signalled by the link word 'however' and then given in the two categories, inevitable and possible, with no ambiguity.

Variety of sentence length within the document can be used by the writer to control the reader's approach. Straightforward facts can be written in comparatively short sentences, perhaps up to 20 words, which can be read quickly. Passages which require more consideration, such as the conclusions of a report, often call for longer sentences, perhaps up to 35 or even 40 words, to slow the reader down and command concentration. Readers are unlikely to notice such manipulation.

▶ Sentences must not be too long: 40 words is a sensible maximum

▶ Variety in sentence length helps the reader

Activity 3.1 Overlong sentence

Divide the very long sentence below into shorter, better-constructed sentences without changing the meaning.

Engineers who work very long hours may suffer long-term effects on their health especially if their work is very intensive and involves responsibility for other people, perhaps younger staff who are less experienced and who need a great deal of supervision and the senior engineers may also be using delicate machinery which requires intense concentration and this state of affairs is also unwise from an employer's point of view because of the risk of accidents.

▶ Sentence construction

We have already looked at two kinds of sentences: those which express one basic idea (simple sentences), and those which express two or more closely related ideas (compound sentences). Some compound sentences can be made up of equal basic units (main clauses) joined by 'and' or 'but' (*never* by a comma alone), while others consist of a main unit and further units which are of lesser importance (subordinate clauses, or phrases).

Knowing the various possible ways of constructing a sentence allows the writer to make decisions. What aspect of the information is to form the main clause of the sentence? The emphasis of the message will depend on the writer's choice. Generally speaking, the first few words of a sentence carry more weight than what follows. In the sentence:

> The machine was overhauled, after which it worked at full capacity.

the main clause is clearly 'The machine was overhauled' and this will be recognised as the most important aspect of the information, especially as it starts the sentence. If the information is changed round, so that we read:

> The machine worked at full capacity after it was overhauled.

the emphasis is now firmly on the fact that the machine worked at full capacity, since this is the main clause and starts the sentence.

This ability to move the emphasis within the sentence is a useful one. We can see the difference between the 'neutral' sentence:

> The machine was badly damaged but it could be repaired.

and two versions which carry different weight:

> The machine could be repaired, although it was badly damaged.

in which the stress is on the repair, and

> The machine was badly damaged, although it could be repaired.

in which the stress is on the damage.

The main clause does not always come at the beginning of the sentence; sometimes we need to emphasise subordinate information, as in:

> Although the repair took six weeks, it was successful.

The stress is on the length of time taken for the repair, as this comes first.

The reader must always be able to identify the main unit of the sentence and recognise where the emphasis has been placed. It is possible for a writer to be so involved with subordinate units that the main unit of the sentence is accidentally left out, as in the following:

> In order to prevent damage to integrated circuits as a result of static discharge which may be caused by a variety of factors such as incorrect handling procedures, poorly grounded instruments or even on occasion by electrostatic buildup on clothes, shoes or floor coverings.

If we try to pick out the main unit of this sentence, we shall soon find that it hasn't got one. 'In order to prevent damage . . .' what must be done? We are not told. Again, we have a sentence more than 40 words long, which is completely out of control. As soon as we identify the main idea in the information and give it a separate sentence:

> Damage to integrated circuits may be the result of static discharge.

the rest falls into place:

> This may result from incorrect handling procedures, poorly grounded instruments or electrostatic buildup on clothes, shoes or floor coverings.

Now that the two sentences have been planned, the redundant details are recognised as such, and removed. 'A variety of factors such as' and 'even on occasion by' add nothing to the meaning; when they have been taken out, we are left with two grammatically correct sentences of 11 and 19 words, an acceptable length.

▶ The main unit (clause) of a sentence conveys the main idea, and must be readily identified by the reader

When the main unit is so identified and the subordinate units are planned, there are still two possible ways in which the sentence as a whole can be organised. The subordinate ideas can be put first, so that they lead up to the main idea. This is a useful technique in writing thrillers, as the tension mounts until the climax is reached:

> As night fell, and with it the hard, driving rain, his determination increased and, breathless, exhausted, running onwards although he no longer knew in what direction, stumbling and nearly falling so that he grazed his hands and twisted his ankle, he now knew more certainly than ever that he would, if need be, die rather than surrender.

Everything in the sentence leads up to that final, dramatic statement that 'he would die rather than surrender', and the impact is made stronger by the buildup of detail: the night, the rain, his exhaustion, loss of sense of direction, pain – *despite all this*, the writer is saying, death was preferable to surrender.

Such is the art of the novelist; the engineer writing technical information must approach the material very differently. The reader must know *at once* what the writer is talking about, so that all the subsidiary ideas can be weighed and considered. Tension is irrelevant. A back-to-front sentence, with the main point at the end, is merely irritating, as in the following two real-life examples:

> Upon removing the packaging materials damage in the form of scratches and abrasions was noted.

The damage is presumably what matters in this sentence, but it need not be spelt out – scratches and abrasions *are* damage, and the reader doesn't need to be told:

> Scratches and abrasions were noted when the packaging was removed.
> (15 words reduced to 10)
> To present detailed waste water proposals in the absence of community structure plans is not possible.

Only at the end of the sentence does the reader get the message: it is not possible. If the sentence is turned round, it becomes clear at once:

> It is impossible to present detailed waste water proposals in the absence of community structure plans.

There is an additional advantage in this ordering of the sentence. 'Present' can in writing, although not in speech, be either a verb ('to presént') or an adjective ('présent'), and we do not know how to interpret it until we understand the context. In the original form of the sentence, we cannot be sure that 'presént' is intended until at least halfway through; in the inverted form of the sentence, we know almost at once.

There is another reason for organising sentences the 'right way round'. The writer wants to attract the reader's attention, and it is unhelpful to leave the most appealing information until the end:

> Further to our discussions and my brief survey, I have pleasure in giving details below of my findings together with approximate indications of the likely savings that might accrue by raising hot water directly in each office at approximately 100% efficiency and saving distribution costs.

The engineer who wrote this real-life sentence had an important message: 'I can increase efficiency and save money.' Who could resist the appeal of such a sentence? This exciting offer is totally hidden in words, buried at the end of a long sentence of 45 words instead of being highlighted:

> In the light of our discussions and my brief survey, I have pleasure in giving my findings. Savings can be made and efficiency increased by raising hot water directly in each office. Details are as follows:

Three ideas are presented: the findings result from discussions and a survey; savings can be made; detailed information follows. The interesting word 'savings' now appears at the start of a sentence, where it is likely to catch the reader's attention.

▶ Start the sentence with the most important idea

Activity 3.2 Organising a sentence

The sentence below comes from a real-life report. It has the ugly start 'due to', which suggests that it is not well organised, and the reader has to read more than half of it in order to know what it is about. Rewrite it, giving emphasis first to the weight of the rigs and then to the need for a tow truck.

Due to their weight, it is necessary to use a tow truck to move the rigs.

Of course, starting with the main idea is just a guideline rather than an absolute rule. Occasionally, for the 'political' reasons which may at times affect an engineer's writing, it might be better to write a back-to-front sentence:

> Your proposal is interesting ... in many ways attractive ... and if the economic climate were different ... but we must regretfully decline ...

The approach is gentle to make the refusal more palatable!

▶ Compound verbs

So far, we have looked at sentences which have a main clause or main clauses and subsidiary units, either phrases which have no verbs, or subordinate clauses introduced by words like 'when', 'although' or 'because'. It has been assumed that the verb can be easily identified, and that it consists of a single word. This is not always so. Verbs can be made up of more than one word: I 'am working', they 'were working'. Both these words are needed if the main clause of the sentence is to make sense. Both are parts of the main verb.

The verb 'am working' is made up of two parts, an auxiliary verb (am) and a participle (working). The auxiliary verb does the work of letting us know the person and the tense of the verb, for example whether I 'am' or they 'are', and whether I 'was' or they 'have been'. The participle, which often ends in 'ing', tells us what action is being taken ('working' rather than 'sitting' or 'writing'). As soon as one part of the verb is missing, the sense is lost. So, for example, we cannot give a message that 'I working on the night shift' (Am I? Was I?) any more than we can convey the meaning by saying 'I am on the night shift' (the reader doesn't know what I'm doing; I could be sleeping!). If the verb consists of more than one word, every word has its part to play in giving the message.

However, if a sentence already contains a complete main verb, in practice we often use just a participle, understanding the missing auxiliary verb. 'Working with the lathe' is clearly neither a main clause nor a full sentence, as it does not make sense. We could make it complete by adding to it: '*I was* working with the lathe.' But the main point of the message might be different: 'I produced a smooth finish.' This is also a main clause/complete sentence. Both sentences have the same subject, I, and for this reason we might choose to bring the two ideas together by omitting 'I was' from the first sentence. Thus 'I was working with the lathe and I produced a smooth finish' becomes:

Working with the lathe, I produced a smooth finish.

This is a correct sentence, with the main unit 'I produced a smooth finish', and a subordinate unit, 'working with the lathe' which does not by itself make sense. We can understand it because the word 'I' is the subject of both the participle and the main verb: *I* am working and *I* produced a smooth finish.

▶ Unrelated participles

However, if the subjects of the participle and of the main verb are different, the result is nonsense:

Working with the lathe, the table had a smooth finish.

The table may have had a smooth finish, but it was not, presumably, working with the lathe! This phenomenon, known as the **unrelated participle**, can produce not only nonsense but also ambiguous humour:

Rusting badly though it was, Jim's brain told him that he would buy the car.

Grammatically, we must assume that Jim's brain, the subject of the main clause, was rusting badly, but nevertheless told him ... We might guess that it was the car which was rusting (but who can be sure?). It is all too easy to produce such sentences:

Used for long periods without ventilation, overheating can cause damage to the instrument.

Is overheating used for long periods, as the sentence says? The intended meaning was probably:

Overheating can cause damage to an instrument which is used for long periods without adequate ventilation.

The auxiliary verb 'is' has now joined its participle 'used', and the sentence makes sense.

▶ Every sentence must have a complete main verb

▶ Split infinitives

A similar problem can arise with the infinitive of the verb (the 'name' of the verb, such as 'to be', 'to work', 'to eat'). The sentence

To drive well, your eyesight must be good.

suggests that your eyesight can drive, well or otherwise. This is clearly nonsense, and so the sentence must be changed:

Your eyesight must be good if you are to drive well.

The verb 'are to drive', a compound verb, is three words long, but all are needed if the sentence is to make sense.

Infinitives are best known for being split. Good style frowns at a word straying between 'to' and the verb: 'to effectively control' is bad, while 'to control effectively' is good. Generally this is true, although, as with many English rules, this one can be broken *if the writer knows why it is being broken*. Emphasis can be thrown on an apparently misplaced word, and such stress may be justified:

To safely remove the radioactive material, it was necessary to call in an expert.

This split infinitive stresses the important word 'safely', and so may be acceptable. Such a device will lose its effectiveness if it is used too often; occasionally and for a clear purpose, it makes its point.

▶ Confused constructions

Some of the problems we have been looking at result from the writer's unwillingness to look at a sentence as a whole:

The run time checks indicate at what point of the process the computer is currently at.

This writer has changed constructions in the middle of the sentence, so that it falls apart. It could be written either as:

The run time checks indicate at what point of the process the computer currently is.

which is awkward, or as:

The run time checks indicate what point of the process the computer is currently at.

This is acceptable, although purists might quibble because the sentence ends with 'at', which sounds clumsy. The difficult word is perhaps 'is', which conveys very little in this sentence. If the writer thinks about the intended message, it could simply be:

The run time checks indicate what point of the process the computer has reached.

which is easier to read and removes the need for 'currently'.

It is always useful for the writer to think of the message in terms of what can sensibly be said, that is, if I had the reader in front of me now, what would I say? The written language is more formal than the spoken language (see Chapter 5 on good style), but once the message has been identified, it can be 'tidied up' for the written form.

I hope to be able to confirm the appointment of James Twigg within the next few days and can assure you that subject to your response to my questions being positive, immediate liaison will be set up between you so that he may be instrumental in arriving at the appropriate conclusions which will benefit us both.

What was the author of this amazing (but real-life) sentence trying to say?

As soon as we've confirmed James Twigg's appointment, which shouldn't take more than a few days, and as long as you're happy with our suggestions, we'll put you in touch with each other. With luck, you'll get on and we'll all do well out of it.

That is too chatty for a written message, but it can be made a little more formal without becoming pompous:

We hope to confirm James Twigg's appointment within a few days. As soon as you have agreed to our suggestions, he will contact you to establish a good working relationship.

The two essential units of information are J.T.'s appointment and J.T.'s making contact. It is obvious that a good working relationship is of benefit to both parties, and there is no point in saying so. A 56-word sentence is replaced by one sentence of 11 words and another of 19 words – only 30 words in all.

▶ Redundant words and phrases

Sentences which ramble, like the one above, can accidentally give misleading information. Again, the essential message must be identified and made clear to the reader.

The lower temperature of 30 degrees Celsius is taken to be the typical external ambient temperature for the equipment in normal use whilst the upper one, 80 degrees Celsius, represents the maximum operational external ambient temperature.

The catch in this sentence is that it mentions 'lower' and 'upper' temperatures, and 'upper' is followed by the word 'maximum'. A careless reader might easily assume that 30 degrees is therefore the minimum, rather than the typical, temperature. The message has to be re-formed without ambiguity (and with 'represents' replaced by 'is'):

> Typically, the equipment will be used at an ambient 30°C. The maximum operational ambient temperature is 80°C.

The key words which are contrasted, 'typically' and 'maximum', are now highlighted at the beginning of the sentences so that no confusion is likely. The temperatures themselves have been abbreviated in a generally recognised way as 30 °C and 60 °C. Each appears at the end of its sentence, so that again the contrast is clear. The unnecessary information 'lower' and 'upper' has been removed, as has the word 'temperature' in the first sentence (what else would 30 °C be?). In the second sentence it is retained for ease of reading.

Redundant words and phrases are common in technical writing. Expressions such as 'Initially, we began by...', 'a new innovation', 'future consequences' (or, more subtly, 'the consequences which lie ahead...'), 'clearly obvious' or 'both the two rivets' all contain unnecessary words. Perhaps the writer is lacking in confidence and feels the need to say the same thing twice. If so, such a message should not be conveyed to the reader. Not only does it suggest hesitation, but it makes the document longer than it need be, which is a waste of time and money.

▶ Write as concisely as possible; omit unnecessary words

Activity 3.3 Redundant words

The following information includes words and phrases that add nothing to the meaning. Rewrite it as briefly and clearly as possible.

The road was originally designed with the needs of residential users predominantly in mind, although over a number of years an element of commercial use, much of which consists of retail properties, has come into existence. If an additional amount of traffic is generated, as it might well be if the current proposal is implemented, problems of increased congestion and even more pollution would inevitably result, to the detriment of residents.

▶ Singular and plural

There are other difficulties with sentence structure which also arise from a lack of planning. A sentence may move from the singular to the plural or vice versa, because the subject is not clearly identified:

> The failure of the systems that we have installed recently have led to the current financial crisis.

The subject of the main verb in this sentence, 'have led', is the singular word 'failure': the form of the verb should therefore also be singular, 'has led'. We can see how this mistake arose. Between the singular word 'failure' and the plural verb 'have led', there is the plural word 'systems' followed correctly by the plural 'we have installed'. Two instances of the plural have led the writer to assume that the verb needed must also be plural, forgetting that the original subject word 'failure' was in fact singular. As a check, the writer should ask, '*what* led to the current financial crisis?' to which the answer is, 'the failure'. The sentence should read:

> The failure of the systems that we have installed recently has led to the current financial crisis.

The word 'each', which is singular, can produce similar difficulties:

> Each of the systems which we have installed recently have given us initial problems.

The subject of 'have given' is 'each', meaning 'each one', and the sentence should thus read:

> Each of the systems which we have installed recently has given us initial problems.

▶ The subject and the verb must agree, both singular or both plural

▶ Expressions to be used with care

Expressions dealt with in this section
It, which, such that/so that

Two other dangerous subject words are 'it' and 'which'. Both are easily attached to the wrong word or phrase; sometimes the reader finds great difficulty in relating them to anything:

The question of how this work should be carried out is one which it is difficult to answer. During our discussions, I said it might be possible to work from a cradle but due to the instability of this type of apparatus, it could prove extremely difficult. Also, due to the large scale of work involved, it would increase the length of the contract.

There are four uses of 'it' in this passage, and none is easily linked to a meaning. Much of the first sentence is redundant in any case; it means no more than 'we are not sure'. In the next sentence, the second 'it' means little more than 'this', and the sentence could be reorganised into a more concise form. The third sentence suffers from the same problems as the second. The passage could be rewritten as:

We are not yet sure how to carry out this work. Using a cradle, as I suggested previously, would be difficult because of its instability. Given the scale of the work, this method would also be time consuming.

'Which' is similarly tricky:

Manuals are mainly held in the print room, but some by individuals which are often unique.

Grammatically, 'which' refers to 'individuals', but there are two problems here:

- individuals are *always* unique
- individuals are people, and therefore referred to as 'who' rather than 'which'.

Common sense, but not grammar, tells us that 'which' refers to 'manuals', and that the sentence should be rearranged to read:

While most manuals are held in the print room, some which are unique [presumably, 'of which there are no copies'] are held by individuals.

An expression much favoured by engineers is 'such that'.

Data have been collected from field surveys such that future projects can be planned.

(For a discussion of the word 'data', see page 17.) In this sentence, 'such' is ambiguous. It may mean 'in such a way that':

Data have been collected from field surveys in such a way that future projects can be planned.

In this case, it is the *method* of collection which has enabled the planning of future projects. However, 'such' may mean 'so that':

> Data have been collected from field surveys so that [= in order that] future projects can be planned.

Here, data were collected and *as a result* it is possible to plan future projects. 'Such that' can, of course, be used correctly:

> The method of collection was such that it enabled future projects to be planned.

In this case, 'such that' means 'of such a type' or 'of such a quality'. This use is comparatively rare, and it is worth checking that 'such that' has not been used when a different meaning was intended.

▶ Negative writing

Perhaps it is a natural diffidence among engineers which encourages them to write in a negative way. Expressions such as 'it is difficult to deny', 'it is not unlikely that' and 'it is not possible to disprove that' suggest that the writer is hesitant (or diffident). Carried to excess, such writing ends up by undermining the reader's confidence:

> If the trend shown continues, then there should be no reason why an improvement in productivity of approaching 40% is not achievable.

This is good news, but the reader might be forgiven for feeling that the outlook is gloomy. 'No reason' followed by 'not achievable' leaves a confused impression. The writer was trying to say:

> If we keep up the good work, we'll just about make a 40% rise in production.

or, more formally:

> If the present trend continues, we should approach a 40% rise in production.

or, to give emphasis to the good news:

> A 40% rise in production is forecast if the present trend continues.

which sounds much more cheerful than the original sentence!
Perhaps negatives are most frequent when the news is bad:

> It is impossible to deny that if the present trend is not reversed, production figures will fail to show the expected rise of 40%.

The writer crowds negatives together (impossible, deny, not reversed, fail to show) presumably so that the reader is led gently to the dismal tidings. Such writing can produce difficult statements:

It is impossible to deny that production figures have not risen.

Presumably this means that we have to admit the truth, but we would much rather not do so.

▶ Plan the sentence so that it says what it means in a positive way

---

Activity 3.4 Overcomplicated writing

Rewrite the following real-life passages, clarifying the meaning and improving the grammar and punctuation.

1. Particular care should be taken to ensure that where an activity has overrun, then that resource requirement for the remainder of that activity is reflected in the current report in addition to the resource needed to maintain the programme during the reporting period.

2. It should be noted that the project group's decision to resume work on the existing prototype in no way indicates any belief in non-feasibility of the other possible methods. The reason for carrying on with the original design being mainly a practical one in that it would seem to be more worthwhile attempting to successfully terminate one approach to the topic rather than start again from scratch using another method and possibly only, with luck, reaching prototype stage.

▶ **Full stops, exclamation marks, question marks**

Full stops are found at the ends of sentences and, although less frequently nowadays, in abbreviations. The sentence which you have just read shows the conventions: a capital letter at the start and a full stop at the end. Engineering writers tend to overlook full stops and use commas instead (see p. 31). This is always wrong, as the following example shows:

Sentences cannot simply be put together, they need a word or phrase that joins them, they should otherwise be separate, the commas should be changed to full stops.

This is a simple example of a common problem. The writer is saying:

Sentences cannot simply be put together.
They need a word or phrase which joins them.
They should otherwise be separate.
The commas should be changed to full stops.

The four sentences above are correct, but dull. Bearing in mind what was said earlier about variety of sentence length (see p. 29), it seems appropriate to use a joining word (conjunction) in one case:

Sentences cannot simply be put together. Either they need a word or phrase which joins them or they should be kept separate. The commas should be changed to full stops.

The first sentence and the third sentence make important points, and have been kept separate to give them emphasis. 'Either...or' is a good way of joining the two sentences which obviously show alternative ways of tackling the sentence problem.

The alternatives to full stops are exclamation marks, question marks and semicolons (which are dealt with separately). Exclamation marks, as their name suggests, show sudden reactions: 'Stop!' 'Look out!' 'That's amazing!' Their use in engineering writing is, to put it mildly, rare.

Question marks, again as one would expect, show the exact words spoken in a question:

How should we tackle this problem?
What results might we expect?

Such questions are usually unhelpful in writing (although often useful in speech) as the writer is about to give the answer. Writers are sometimes tempted to use questions as headings:

What conclusions can be drawn from this evidence?

Again, this is not helpful to the reader, and is usually considered to be poor style (in any case, the one heading 'Conclusions' is generally sufficient – see p. 72). The only person who is going to answer the question is the writer who asked it, and so why bother? Occasionally, a series of questions can be used to draw attention to what the reader would want to ask, each question being followed by an appropriate answer:

How does the machine work?
It works by ...

How much does it cost?
The basic cost is . . .
What about maintenance?
A thorough overhaul has to be carried out . . .

As the above example suggests, this technique is usually applied in sales literature, or, sometimes effectively, in basic instruction manuals; it is not appropriate in, for example, a technical report.

Full stops used to appear in abbreviations, of either the 'name' variety (such as U.N.I.C.E.F.) or the Latin original variety (such as e.g. or i.e.). This is now rare, and although it is still correct, the modern convention allows the initials to run together (UNICEF, eg, ie). If there is any chance of misunderstanding, then it is better to write the term in full (as in the case of litres, when an abbreviation to the single 'l' can be misread). If a company or organisation maintains full stops in its title, then of course they should be used.

▶ Semicolons

Semicolons may also take the place of full stops. If two sentences are closely related in subject matter, perhaps by contrast or a common factor, the relationship can be stressed by joining the sentences with a semicolon:

The design of the bridge was superb at the time; today it has to carry too much heavy traffic.

Each 'sentence' remains an accurate, grammatical whole, making sense by itself. However, the link of information (then . . . now) is strong, and is emphasised by the use of a semicolon instead of a full stop at the end of the first sentence (followed by a small, not a capital, letter). This use of the semicolon can produce an elegant style; if it is not overused, it can be most effective.

Semicolons can also be used to separate sections of information in a list:

The following hazards must be considered:

1. insulation and protection from electric shock;
2. possible fire risks and the location of fire extinguishers;
3. testing of pressurised or other highly stressed components.

Nowadays, these semicolons are often omitted, which is acceptable as long as the individual items in the list are short; if they are more than a line in length, then for clarity the punctuation should be retained.

▶ Colons

Colons are not interchangeable with semicolons. The most common use of a colon is to introduce an example, as we have seen in this book, or introduce a quotation, as in the case of the following extract from the author's *Technical Report Writing*, an IEE Guide (Institution of Electrical Engineers, September 2001 edition, page 14):

> Short sentences produce a clear, easily-read style for factual material. Information which needs to be considered and held in tension with other information is better given in longer sentences which slow the reader down. No reader wants to be brought to a standstill by a sentence which is eight lines long.

A colon may also introduce a list, as in the following example:

> The equipment needed for this test is as follows:

- oscilloscope
- digital voltmeter
- signal generator
- logic analyser
- power supplies
- soldering iron.

Note that as the items in this list are all very short, they are not followed by punctuation apart from the final full stop.

A list may sometimes simply be an amplification of the preceding information:

> There are three main types of stepping motor: variable reluctance motors, permanent magnet motors and hybrid motors.

This is a short list, not printed in a list format and containing only three items, but the first eight words serve as an introduction to the items which follow.

Colons used to be followed by a dash (:–), but the dash is usually omitted nowadays.

▶ Commas

In some ways, commas are a difficult form of punctuation, because while they often follow rules, to a certain extent they are also the result of individual choice, of a feeling for the language.

The most common use of a comma is to separate the main part of a sentence from a subordinate part (see p. 31), either to make the meaning clear or allow the reader to 'take breath' naturally. This is an important aspect of the use of commas, as the 'natural pause' in a long sentence helps the reader to assimilate the information given so far and prepare for what is to come. The division within a sentence can be clearly seen in the following:

When the bridge was first built, it was adequate for traffic requirements.

If we read this sentence aloud, we shall pause naturally at the end of the subordinate unit (after the word 'built') before moving on to the main part of the sentence. The sequence can, of course, be reversed:

The bridge was adequate for traffic requirements, when it was first built.

We may not feel the need for a comma after 'requirements'(the 'feeling' for language), but as soon as the subordinate unit becomes longer, we need the comma again to allow us a brief pause:

The bridge was originally adequate for traffic requirements, but today there are frequent holdups and sometimes long queues stretching back towards the motorway.

The subordinate unit, as we have seen, may appear neither at the beginning nor at the end of the sentence, but in the middle:

The bridge, originally adequate for traffic requirements, is today the scene of frequent holdups and the cause of long queues.

The phrase 'originally adequate for traffic requirements' is now enclosed by two commas, so that it is separated from the main sentence, which would, indeed, make sense without it. Both commas are necessary; if one is left out, the sentence will not read correctly.

We have just seen a different but related use of the comma:

The main sentence would, indeed, make sense without it.

In this case, one word, 'indeed', is between commas. It is a comment on the rest of the sentence and could be left out without a change of meaning. Many expressions such as 'on the other hand', 'nevertheless', 'in spite of . . .' can be used in this way:

There is, however, a plan to build a second bridge over the river.
Nevertheless, for the time being the problem will remain.
It is possible to avoid the long queues, however.
The detour needed, it must be remembered, is lengthy.

From these examples, we can see that the 'comment' words and phrases are separated from the rest of the sentence by a comma or commas, depending on where the comment is placed in the sentence. There is a modern tendency to leave out one or both commas, with ambiguous results:

> The bridges, which cross the river, are in urgent need of repair.
> The bridges which cross the river are in urgent need of repair.

The first sentence means that *all* the bridges cross the river and are in need of repair, while the second sentence means that *only* the bridges which cross the river are in need of repair (those over the railway line are in good order). The test for the writer is to read the two sentences out loud, and the natural pauses of the speaking voice will make the difference of meaning clear. In writing, we have to depend on the presence or absence of the commas to show us which is meant.

One more case of 'comment' words or phrases is worth noting. Sometimes in introducing a person or a book, article and so on, we add an explanatory comment:

> James Twigg, an engineer who works locally, came to the meeting.
> James Twigg, chairman of the local branch of the institution, came to the meeting.
> James Twigg's book, which has been so well reviewed, will be on sale after the meeting.
> *Modern Bridge Design,* by James Twigg, is on sale now.

The same rules apply as for the other comment words and phrases: a comma before and after separates the comment from the rest of the sentence.

Commas can also be used to separate short items in a list, when they are written within the text rather than listed down the page:

> In digital electronic hardware testing, the engineer makes use of an oscilloscope, a dvm, a signal or pulse generator and a logic analyser.

There is not usually a comma before the 'and' at the end of the list (but see below).

The main uses of commas in technical writing have now been discussed. The remaining uses are less important, but it is worth noting that commas are used before or after direct speech:

> He said, 'I shall cross the bridge.'
> 'I shall cross the bridge,' he said.

There are also commas which are placed to help the reader, for instance the comma before 'and' (usually forbidden in school!). If the sense is made clearer by the comma, then it should be used:

I crossed the bridge and the mountains lay all before me.

The reader might well understand, 'I crossed the bridge and the mountains', and then have to readjust the reading as it becomes clear that the sentence continues. A comma makes all plain:

I crossed the bridge, and the mountains lay all before me.

Sometimes, two or more uses of 'and' in a sentence have different values:

I crossed the flat marsh land and then the bridge and at last the vast and beautiful mountains came into sight.

This sentence contains three versions of 'and'. The first and the third are comparatively unimportant, linking related ideas. Indeed, 'vast and beautiful' is almost to be understood as one expression. The voice's natural pause comes after 'bridge' and that is where the comma should be:

I crossed the flat marsh land and then the bridge, and at last the vast and beautiful mountains came into sight.

The effect of leaving out such commas can be ambiguous:

I went to the meeting with Jim and Sarah and Peter came later.

When this sentence is spoken, the natural inflection of the voice makes the meaning clear, but when we read it we have no idea whether I went with Jim and Sarah (Peter was late) or whether I went with Jim only (Sarah and Peter were both late). A comma reinforcing the important 'and' (that is, after either 'Jim' or 'Sarah') makes the sentence unambiguous. It is in fact reflecting the pattern of the spoken sentence, which is often the job of a comma.

The voice has been used as a guide several times in this section, and it is a good one. If in doubt, read the passage aloud and notice where the voice pauses naturally. Mark the place with a comma.

▶ Quotation marks

Quotation marks are used less than they used to be. For quotations which are longer than one line of text, convention indicates that the writer should start a new line, indenting the words quoted and going back to the left-hand margin at the end of the quotation. This style was followed in the quotation about the importance of sentence length on page 46. However, shorter quotations must still be acknowledged as such, and for that purpose quotation marks are needed. The normal practice is to use the single form round the words quoted:

> Earlier in this book, (p. 3), it was stated that, in writing, 'shock tactics apparently work, but are not recommended'. We want the reader to concentrate on the message rather than to be distracted by a gimmick of the writer.

All quotations must be acknowledged in the text (see p. 98).

▶ Dashes and brackets

Asides, comments or examples may be placed between dashes – as in this sentence – as an alternative to commas. Dashes tend to be informal in style and should be avoided in technical writing, especially when there is mathematical information included. It is too easy for a dash to be read as a minus sign.

Brackets, on the other hand, are 'heavy' punctuation. They break up the flow of the reading, and should be used only when the information which they enclose is not an integral part of the sentence. Notes like (see Figure 6.1) perhaps show one of the two most common uses of brackets, the other being to enclose an abbreviation immediately after the first use of the full term (see p. 94 for more information about abbreviations). However, irony or personal comment may be shown in this way, as in a previous sentence about commas:

> There are also commas which are placed to help the reader, for instance the comma before 'and' (usually forbidden in school!).

Such a use is obviously rare in technical material. In any case, too many brackets on the page look unwieldy and dull.

(If the writer has to include complex mathematical information, including different shapes and sizes of brackets, an equation editor such as that produced by Microsoft should be employed – see page 97.)

▶ Hyphens

Hyphens are sometimes confused with dashes, but they are shorter (- rather than –) and have different uses. They may be used to bring together two words which gain a new meaning from being joined: 're-cover' is different from 'recover', 'cross-section' is different from 'cross section'. The hyphen may give emphasis to the idea of repetition ('make and re-make' stresses the 're' aspect), or, most importantly, it may be used to help the reader ('re-emerge' is easier to recognise than 'reemerge'). This last usage has a major impact on the flow of the writing; if the reader has to readjust to the reading on a regular basis, the action of reading is slowed down and made uncomfortable. The modern tendency is to omit hyphens wherever possible, and this is often carried too far. While the disappearance of the hyphen from a word like cooperate or subcontract is unlikely to cause problems, other words such as reallife (real-life) simply look peculiar and are sometimes unrecognisable. Whenever the reader will read a word more readily because it has a hyphen, the careful writer will provide one.

Many new words start by including hyphens, and then by convention become one word, such as online, bandwidth, wordprocessor (this last being seen also as two separate words, 'word processor'). Such words rarely cause a problem once their form has been established. Word-breaks (an example of a useful hyphen) occur when a word is divided between two lines of text, although this is of course rare nowadays unless the material is produced in narrow columns. However, if such a word-break does occur, a hyphen can be used to bring the join to the reader's attention, especially if word which is divided can be read as two separate words ('rearrange' being seen as 'rear range', or 'legend', entertainingly, becoming 'leg end').

Scientific and technical terms often contain hyphens which reflect two aspects of the meaning. Such words include vacuum-sealed, three-dimensional and single-track. There are many others. The meaning depends on the hyphen, and it should never be omitted. The following sentence is not easy to read, largely because it is not immediately obvious which words belong together:

The insulation is made of glass reinforced foil faced mineral wool.

As soon as hyphens are added, the meaning is clearer:

The insulation is made of glass-reinforced foil-faced mineral wool.

▶ Apostrophes

Apostrophes produce more headaches than any other form of punctuation. They are either overused, in words which happen to be plurals ending in 's' or ignored altogether, even when this creates ambiguity.

There are two uses of an apostrophe:

- to show where a letter or letters have been omitted
- to show possession.

The former use is rare in technical writing, as it is informal in style. It might appear in a note to a colleague or an email message:

> Please let Jim know that I can't be at the meeting tomorrow. I've got to be on the plane for New York by lunchtime.

As a note for a colleague, this is acceptable, and the abbreviations 'can't' and 'I've' are appropriate. 'Can't' is a shortened form of 'cannot', and the apostrophe shows where 'no' is omitted. Similarly, 'ha' is omitted from 'I have', leaving 'I've'. This is the spoken language and also the informal written language. In most professional writing, such words must be spelt out in full: 'it is', not 'it's'. ('It's', the abbreviation for 'it is' or 'it has', takes the apostrophe because of the omitted letters).

The second use of the apostrophe is more difficult. It identifies the owner of an object, as in 'the engineer's logbook'. It will also show if there is more than one owner, as in 'the engineers' logbook', which indicates that the logbook in question is shared by more than one engineer. Generally, in English, the apostrophe is before the 's' in the singular and after the 's' in the plural, as in this example.

There are exceptions, however. Some words do not add 's' to make the plural but use what we might think of as a different form of the word, the most common group of such words being 'men, women, children, people'. These words are already plural, and so they have the apostrophe before the 's': men's overcoats, women's shoes, children's bicycles, people's opinions. There are other eccentric forms of plural, such as changing 'y' into 'ies', as in secretary, secretaries. It would be difficult to write 'secretaries's', and so the final 's' is dropped, as in 'secretaries' desks'.

There is one group of words which suggests possession but which *never* has an apostrophe. These words follow the pattern of a verb (I have, you have, and so on):

> mine, thine, his, hers, its, ours, yours, theirs

'Its', meaning 'belonging to it' does *not* have an apostrophe. This is the word that causes most confusion, because of its two forms, as shown in the sentence:

It's my car that has its lights on.

The first 'it's' means 'it is' and so takes the apostrophe, while the second indicates possession ('the lights belonging to it') and so does not have an apostrophe. The best way to remember this distinction is to ask: does 'it's' mean 'it has' or 'it is'? If the answer is no, there is no apostrophe. It's as simple as that!

Many writers are so uncomfortable with the apostrophe that they leave it out altogether. Usually this is not important, and it is perhaps better than having a sprinkling of unnecessary apostrophes on the page. However, occasionally the position of the apostrophe changes the meaning:

Our client's money has disappeared from the bank.
Our clients' money has disappeared from the bank.

In the first case, only one client is going to be angry; in the second, we are going to be faced with more than one client, perhaps hordes of angry clients. Only the position of the apostrophe will show which.

Fortunately, there is a rule of thumb for deciding whether an apostrophe has been correctly placed. Write the word out, including the apostrophe. Then cover the apostrophe and everything that follows it. Ask two questions: is what is left a sensible English word, and is it what you intend to say? If the answer to both questions is yes, then the apostrophe is in the right place. For instance, if we want to write:

There is a problem with the secretary's computer.

and we apply the rule, we are left with the word 'secretary', a perfectly good singular word. If that is meant, the apostrophe is correct. If, however, the problem extended to the computers of several secretaries, we might be tempted to write 'secretarie's computers'; applying the rule would produce the nonsense word 'secretarie', which is clearly wrong. The position of the apostrophe can then be corrected to:

There is a problem with the secretaries' computers.

For reasons of style, it is sometimes better to turn an expression round to avoid the apostrophe. 'The book's pages' is ugly, while 'the pages of the book' sounds more attractive. This inversion is often a useful device, although it is a good idea to say the expression aloud first and listen to how it sounds. Choose whichever form sounds more natural. It may be the 'of the' form, which has the added bonus of allowing the hesitant writer to dispense with the dreaded apostrophe.

Activity 3.5 Punctuation

Add or correct the punctuation in the following passage.

Businesspeople are more likely to take the train it seems if the total journey time is three hours or less however if its longer they will consider flying it's a pity that train journeys are so often plagued by mobile phones an everincreasing menace especially to those who would like a quiet journey on which to read use their laptops or in extreme cases go to sleep at least nowadays there is the occasional quiet coach where its possible to escape from the mobile and its noisy users

---

► **Summary**

- ► Sentences contain one idea, or two or three closely related ideas which must be correctly joined together
- ► Sentences must not be too long: 40 words is a sensible maximum
- ► Variety in sentence length helps the reader
- ► The main unit (clause) of a sentence conveys the main idea, and must be readily identified by the reader
- ► Start the sentence with the most important idea
- ► Every sentence must have a complete main verb
- ► Write as concisely as possible; omit unnecessary words
- ► The subject and the verb must agree, both singular or both plural
- ► Plan the sentence so that it says what it means in a positive way

4 Paragraphs and formats

As we have seen, sentences contain at least one major idea (main clause, which makes sense by itself), often with subordinate aspects (clauses or phrases) added to it (see p. 24). Paragraphs are developed from a collection of ideas, all of which are linked by a central theme.

▶ Definition of a paragraph

A paragraph may be formed from a single extended idea or a series of ideas, united by theme and creating an organised and logical passage of text. This is obviously not as rigid a definition as that of a sentence in the previous chapter: there are fewer rules about paragraph writing. Nevertheless, a text without paragraphs is difficult to read. Pages of closely printed information, with no breaks or spaces, are overwhelming, and the reader will find it almost impossible to follow a logical flow of ideas, even if it exists. The end of a paragraph allows a breathing space in which readers can make sure that a set of ideas has been understood and assimilated before they move on to the next theme. Paragraphs also serve to break up the page and so encourage readers to read on.

▶ Paragraph length

Paragraphs are varied in length, according to the subject matter and the format chosen. Generally speaking, three or four paragraphs to a page look satisfactory in terms of both assimilating a reasonable amount of information, and space. However, emails, letters and reports tend to have shorter paragraphs than articles or books: emails often consist of just one or two paragraphs, letters may have five or six to the page, and reports about the same, although the structure of a report (see p. 72) may dictate a different number.

There is an apparent conflict: paragraph length is dictated both by unity of theme and appearance on the page. In practice, this dual criterion is not a serious problem. Writers who are aware of the importance of presentation can usually plan a paragraph so that it achieves unity. The long paragraphs sometimes found in engineering reports can often be subdivided into two or three separate themes with a common thread running through them. Links between paragraphs will clarify the organisation for the reader, and are themselves a feature of good style (see p. 103).

The theme of a paragraph must be clear, and can often be expressed in a short sentence at the beginning, and perhaps also, in different words, as a summing up at the end. This theme is then developed, explained and clarified by means of technical details, examples or analogies, or even undermined by the ideas expressed in the other sentences. As the writer completes the examination of one theme and moves on to the next, a new paragraph marks the transition for the reader.

▶ Numbering systems

In some writing, it is appropriate to number paragraphs. A letter, for instance, may deal with several topics, each discussed in a paragraph. Numbering will make the material easier to use, as the engineer who is dealing with the information can not only tick each paragraph as it is dealt with, but can also use the same numbers in any further correspondence. Some reports have a system of paragraph numbering (see p. 73), but this is helpful mostly in short reports which are discussed at meetings or over the telephone. (Some organisations demand a paragraph numbering system, in which case staff have no option but to comply; a more helpful system is suggested later in this chapter on page 73.)

▶ Unity of theme

It is already clear that paragraphs have to be planned. If we take the preceding paragraph as an example, we can see that the short opening sentence contains the theme: paragraphs are sometimes numbered. The following sentence gives an example of a case in which numbering is appropriate, and the sentence after that suggests two ways in which such numbering will help the engineer. Another instance of numbered paragraphs is then introduced, and the paragraph ends with a reservation about this particular use. A new theme, the planning of paragraphs, is then introduced in a new paragraph, with the linking statement that 'It is already clear...'.

There are many different ways of organising information, but the basic guideline is: identify the theme and keep related information in the same paragraph, with the proviso that the length of that paragraph should not become unwieldy. Make the theme clear to the reader, preferably at the start, and show the transition to a new theme by starting a new paragraph.

▶ Paragraphs have unity of theme

▶ Good paragraphing produces space on the page and encourages the reader

In passing, we should notice that some paragraphs contain only one sentence, which is all that can be said about the subject. Letters often conclude with sentence-paragraphs, such as:

I look forward to hearing from you.

There is no more to be said, and so these seven words form a complete, correct paragraph (see p. 68).

▶ Lists

A list may break up a paragraph, giving more space on the page and helping the reader to assimilate the ideas one at a time. This device is particularly useful when information has to be remembered for future use (perhaps in an examination!). It would not be particularly easy to learn the following:

> Preventive maintenance should be considered when the time interval between equipment breakdown can be predicted with reasonable accuracy, or when the cost of preventive maintenance attention is less than the repair cost when both costs include that of any lost production. It may also be appropriate when equipment failure is likely to disrupt subsequent production operations or cause customer dissatisfaction. A particularly important application is in cases when injury could result from equipment breakdown.

The first sentence in particular is very long and contains too much information. Although the paragraph has unity of theme, the need for preventive maintenance, it is congested with detail and difficult to take in. However, in the form in which it appears in J D Radford's *The Engineer in Society* (Macmillan, 1984, p. 197), the same information is set out much more clearly:

> . . . preventive maintenance should be considered when the following conditions apply.
>
> 1. The time interval between equipment breakdown can be predicted with reasonable accuracy.
> 2. The cost of preventive maintenance attention is less than the repair cost when both costs include that of any lost production.
> 3. Equipment failure is likely to disrupt subsequent production operations or cause customer dissatisfaction.
> 4. Injury could result from equipment breakdown.

The list is easier to read and remember than the same information written in a long paragraph.

▶ Organisation and layout of lists

There are two basic forms of list:

- those in which individual items are simply 'bulleted' for identification
- those which are either numbered or lettered.

On the whole, the former style is used when the order in which the points are read or dealt with is immaterial (a list of items of equipment might fall into this category), while the latter emphasises the order in which the information is given (for instance, stages in a process, which should always be numbered). Lists are, however, also numbered in order to allow cross-reference to specific items, or, as in the example above, to help the reader who needs to memorise the information.

▶ List information whenever it is possible to do so

If a paragraph contains figures, measurements or dates, the planning stage includes checking exactly what information should be highlighted. Numbers might be better in tabulated form, or a comparison may be drawn by using 'parallel' sentences. In the following paragraph, there is an implicit comparison, but it is difficult to identify the details:

It is interesting to note that between January 2001 and March 2001, 1350 pcb were produced with nine operators, while between January and March 2002, seven operators produced 2869 pcb.

This can be rewritten more clearly as a mini-table:

January–March 2001: 9 operators produced 1350 pcb (150 per operator)
January–March 2002: 7 operators produced 2869 pcb (409.8 per operator)

The dates, number of operators and increased production figures are now easily identified and compared.

▶ Set out numbers in a way which is easy to use

Layout is important in both the planning of paragraphs and the organisation of whole documents. In the rest of this chapter, we look at some of the conventional formats which engineers use regularly in their working lives: email, letters and faxes, reports, specifications and sets of instructions.

▶ Use a conventional format with which the reader is familiar

▶ Emails

In the last few years, emails have become one of the most common means of communication, used within families, between friends and colleagues, within companies and to clients and customers worldwide. In fact, memos have just about died out, faxes and formal letters are used much less frequently, and emails rule under almost any circumstances. They have enormous advantages, in that they can be sent and received at a time convenient to sender and recipient (much more convenient in this way than the telephone); they can be used on the screen or printed out and used as documents; they travel quickly round the world; they can be long or short and can include attachments; they can be sent to individuals or groups as required. They also – this might seem a trivial advantage, but it is nevertheless a benefit under most circumstances – do away with the need for envelopes, stamps and the journey to the post office.

Emails sound like the ideal communication medium, but, as with any new development, people are not always sure how to use them, and few conventions have had time to become established. They also have their own built-in problems: most people receive an infuriating amount of 'spam' (material which was not requested and is not wanted; this may simply be commercial, but can also cause distress, for instance if it is pornographic); security is a constant problem for companies, as hackers have been known to break into highly confidential systems; emails are also liable to virus attack, which can destroy not only the emails on the computer but the hard disk itself, and viruses can be transmitted innocently by senders who are not aware of the infection. There are no complete answers to these problems, although a whole new industry has developed which is working on possible solutions.

Various aspects of email communication will be discussed in this chapter, but it is worth remembering that because emails are such a recent development, conventions could change quickly, especially if companies decide to produce their own guidelines.

Style and tone

There are rules and conventions in writing a business letter which have developed over centuries (see pp. 65–70), but few conventions in an email. One of the most common problems is that writers tend to regard an email as a form of speech: they can be informal, humorous, aggressive or chatty as if they were talking to the recipient, and the speed at which the email travels increases this illusion. The words on the screen, however, are not supported by facial expression or tone of voice: they are simply written words, and that is how the reader sees them. Any attempt to reproduce the habits of speech is likely to fail or be misinterpreted, for instance capital letters used for emphasis may seem aggressive to the reader. Emotions (or 'smilies') are also totally inappropriate in professional writing.

There is a further problem with emails in the context of work. A friendly, informal email between colleagues can be printed out and passed on as a document, and what was intended as a casual exchange of information has become a formal written statement, seen by other people not perhaps known to the originator. If an email is used at work, it must be sufficiently formal to be used as a document, in other words, slang, chattiness, a spoken language approach are not appropriate. The abbreviated language often used in text messages ('u' for 'you', for example) must be avoided for the same reasons. The writer must remember that an email is not necessarily one-to-one communication, even if it starts out with this intention; it can easily turn into written form and be read by many other people.

Nevertheless, emails are often less formal than business letters, and, provided the warning in the previous paragraph is kept in mind, this seems acceptable. Abbreviations such as 'don't' or 'can't' are freely used and the style tends to be friendly in tone rather than stiff and formal. However, if an email is sent to a group of people, its style must be appropriate for all of them, even if some are known to the writer and others are not, some senior in the organisation and others not. Emails may be passed on electronically again and again, and so even if the message is not printed out, it can still reach people whom the writer was not aware of when he or she wrote the message originally.

▶ Emails are not conversational; they can be printed out and turned into documents

Sending an email is an extremely rapid and irreversible process. If the writer is angry or upset, the tone of the message may show this all too clearly; if the sender is extremely angry with the recipient, the email may be violent and offensive, and the reader may well respond, equally rapidly, in the same way. Working relationships can be permanently damaged. If the people concerned had seen one another, they might have retained some human sympathy or willingness to compromise; if they had had to dictate a letter, someone else might have counselled different words; if they had had to take the time to walk to the post office or even the post room, they might have calmed down. Instant communication without the benefit of human contact can allow an unpleasant situation to escalate at high speed. The moral is: if you feel emotional when you start to write an email, do something else first and allow yourself time to think rationally abut the consequences of what you want to say.

Greeting the reader

There are conventions about how to address the reader of a business letter (see p. 66), but none has yet developed for emails. There should always be some form of signing on and signing off: a message with neither a greeting nor a signature is often seen as discourteous. If the recipient is not known to the writer, a letter-type greeting (Dear...) can be used, although it looks oddly formal and out of place in an email (as does 'Yours sincerely'). It is reasonable to start just with the recipient's name on a line by itself before the message begins. If the writer knows the reader well, 'Hello' and the name can be used; 'Hi' is not uncommon, but beware of the difficulty discussed above, that if the email is printed out and passed on, this may look too casual.

There is almost a convention for the end of the message: most emails end with 'Regards', which is pleasant and neither particularly formal nor informal. 'Best wishes' or 'Thank you' might serve when they are appropriate.

Content

Emails can have as much or as little technical content as the situation requires; they can include diagrams or a full report, and so are just as flexible as a business letter with enclosures. However, the text can lose its format in transmission, and so it is wise to send any formatted material as an attachment rather than in the body of the email, always with a brief covering message. If it is essential that every detail is correct, it might be wise to send a hard copy in the post as backup.

Organisations have complex security systems for their electronic communication, using codes, passwords and other tools to make sure that their confidential material is seen only by the intended reader. Even so, emails can be tampered with, or, perhaps more often, passed on inadvertently to a third party, and every engineering writer needs to be particularly careful in transmitting confidential material through this medium.

In sending a long document by email attachment, the writer has to decide whether to number the pages in the way that pages of a technical report are normally numbered. This is a tricky decision, as the length of the pages might be different on the receiver's printer, and the page numbers might therefore be confusing. Nevertheless, if hundreds of pages spill out of the printer and they are not numbered, there is the potential for a serious problem: the writer once left her printer to print out what she assumed was a short document while she went for coffee, only to discover on her return that the office floor was carpeted with paper. There was an unpleasant moment before she realised that the pages were numbered!

Checking emails

It is easy to forget to check an email. Engineers and others, who would not dream of sending a report or business letter without checking it carefully for accuracy of material and keyboarding, will send off an email without even looking it through. Mistakes will give the wrong information and undermine the credibility of the writer just as much in an email as in a more traditional form of communication. If the information is long and/or complex, check from a printout, not just on the screen. Grammar, punctuation and spelling have the same impact at the receiving end as they would have on the printed page, which is where, in any case, the text may end up.

There is an extra level of checking in an email: making sure that the right people receive the information. If an email is sent to a group, the writer must check that every individual in the group *should* (because of eligibility and the nature of the content) receive the message. It has been known for a complaint about a colleague to travel to the person concerned simply because he or she was on the circulation list. In a lengthy exchange of emails, the message itself gets longer and longer, and material at the beginning may be forgotten by the writers; incidentally, if the exchange is received by a third party, they may assume that it has been completed before it has, simply because what they see on the screen is signed off and looks like the end of the communication.

Emails are part of everyday life, and very useful, too. Nevertheless, most organisations can probably cite instances of their misuse and the serious consequences in terms of client relations that can result from the simple assumption that an email is a form of speech; it isn't. An email is written and can form part of a larger document and travel in directions of which the original writer would never dream.

Activity 4.1 Email

The following material was written by a tutor to engineering student 'project managers', and sent to the group as an email attachment. The essential information is included, but it is not easy to follow or use. It needs to be organised and written in a consistent and appropriate style.

Subject: Year 1 projects: safety

I need to know the hazards which are associated with your project, remembering that if you take apparatus away from supervised areas

(Cont'd)

special precautions are necessary. Let me know the steps you propose to deal with them. Watch out for: electric shock and insulation and protection, fire risks and where you intend to keep fire extinguishers and other fire-fighting equipment; if pressurised or other highly stressed components are involved they must be protected against; moving components must be guarded, such as rotating shafts, gears, belts, pulleys; you may also be injured by falling or tripping especially if there are sharp projections or objects are dropped. The first time hazardous apparatus is used, your project supervisor must be present and if it is very hazardous, every time. If you have problems with safety, I will assist you.

▶ Faxes

The place of the formal business letter has, in recent years, been steadily eroded, by greater use of the telephone and the popularity of email. The former is outside the scope of this book (but see Further Reading, p. 143); the latter presents, as we have seen, a particularly interesting challenge. The fax is used less frequently nowadays, but it is worth looking briefly at some of its conventions before the place of the business letter is discussed.

Formal faxes

The formal fax is still used by many organisations in place of a letter, especially to convey complex material which is not, for some reason, held online. A photocopy of a diagram, for instance, can be faxed to the recipient. Clearly, it saves time, the cost of postage and the trouble of ensuring that the sender catches the post. Reasonable confidentiality can now be built in and the fax can be linked directly to a computer for convenience. Yet writers are inclined to forget that if the fax is replacing a letter, it should have the safeguards of a letter: it should be carefully printed out, checked and, if appropriate, countersigned. It should certainly be treated with the same respect.

The situation is helped if the company has produced a well laid out cover-sheet, to be used for all formal faxes. This will give the name and status or department of the sender, together with the company name and logo, address, telephone and fax numbers. The sender's direct line for telephone and fax, and email address, should be added if appropriate.

Similar information should be given for the recipient, not least to ensure that the fax reaches its intended destination as quickly as possible. The date and the number of pages should be given, and a short heading to highlight the subject. If all this is well designed, the fax can be as impressive as the company's business letters.

In style, the formal fax will be similar to any other business correspondence which goes outside its own organisation, although even this has changed subtly over the years. Letters have become much less formal than they used to be and pompous letters (starting with 'I am in receipt of yours of the 6th ult.' or some such horror) are a thing of the past (*almost!*). Letters have also become shorter, being used nowadays much less to convey a great deal of technical detail and much more as a brief introduction to, or overview of, the subject (the covering letter). It is much more common for detailed information to be presented separately as a report.

Informal faxes

Email has overtaken the fax for the transmission of quick answers to brief questions. Nevertheless, the fax is still used when the material to be conveyed is not immediately available in electronic form and when scanning it is not an easy option. The cover-sheet mentioned above should still be used, but as the communication is generally one to one, further conventions are hardly necessary. If the fax is handwritten, however, it is worth using black ink and a pen with a medium rather than a fine point, or else the image received might not be clear enough to be read accurately.

▶ Letters

There are, in spite of technical advances in the means of communication, many occasions which still demand a letter. Contact with individual staff, such as appointment, promotion, changes in working conditions or formal disciplinary action, is in letter form. Engineers may have to write to members of the general public or influential groups, for instance to ask for permissions, and of course any technical report is likely to be sent with a covering letter.

In preparing to write any of these, or other, letters, the engineer needs to assemble useful information: technical data, previous letters on the same subject and up-to-date or revised details which must be included. It is helpful to look at the last letter received from the company to which the present letter is addressed, not only to make sure that all relevant topics are covered in the reply, but also to check the tone used. If the reader's company uses a formal style and formal names, it is generally wise to follow suit and vice versa; it would suggest disagreement and perhaps hostility to write 'Dear Mr Twigg' when he signed his letter 'Jim'.

Forms of address

The use of first names is a tricky subject. Business letters once began 'Dear Sir' or 'Dear Sirs' as a matter of course. Although this is still not uncommon, surnames are now more widely used ('Dear Mr Twigg') and first names ('Dear Jim') are also common, even among people who have not actually met, or even had any previous connection. There is still need for caution. Jim, whom you know well, may be away from the office and your letter may instead be dealt with by Tom, whom you do not know. Worse, Jim may, no doubt by oversight, have failed to pay his bills, and it is difficult to write a stiff letter threatening legal action if you begin it, as usual, with 'Dear Jim'. Discretion is needed, and previous correspondence is a useful guide to what is appropriate. Company policy, of course, may be the overriding factor.

Engineers may be men or women. This seemingly obvious fact is sometimes overlooked by letter writers, and too many letters still start with 'Dear Sir', when a little research would have shown that 'Sir' is female. People are often unsure about the correct form of address to a woman, and indeed the situation is changing and the conventions are not entirely clear. 'Dear Madam' is as appropriate as 'Dear Sir', although, oddly, it sounds rather more formal; 'Dear Miss Twigg' or 'Dear Mrs Twigg' is sometimes resented, and indeed a woman's married state, being irrelevant to the competence of her engineering, is often not shown. 'Dear Ms Twigg' is generally acceptable, as is 'Dear Jane Twigg'. It is helpful for women engineers to print their names under the signature in the form which they would like to receive in reply (another good reason for checking previous correspondence), and the full-name signature, as opposed to initial and surname, at least prevents the 'Dear Mr Twigg' response. In passing, it is worth noting that an increasing number of women use their maiden names for professional purposes, thus adding to the confusion. It is worth taking trouble to find out other useful details about the recipient of a letter: first name or initial (needed on the envelope if not in the letter) and job title.

Layout of letters

Most organisations have templates for letters, and these should obviously be used. However, individuals still have to write letters from time to time, and the conventional layout of a letter is nowadays like this.

LETTER FORMAT

(a) 23 Grange Road
Upper Woodedge Avenue
Mistleton
North Sussex
MT 74 6DL

(b) 17 January 2005

(c) FOA **Ms J Mason**

Courses Unit
IEE
Michael Faraday House
Six Hills Way
Stevenage
Herts
SG1 2AY

(d) Dear Ms Mason

(e) Technical writing course

(f) I understand that your Courses Unit holds two day courses in Technical Writing, and I should be grateful if you would kindly send me details, together with an indication of the cost, venues and dates in the next three months.

The organisation for which I work is too small to have its own training programme, and I am anxious to improve my writing skills, especially in preparing specifications. I am a member of the Institution.

My email address is richard.pl.jones@hotmail.com

(g) I look forward to hearing from you.

(h) Yours sincerely

(i) *Richard P L Jones*

(j) R P L Jones, Senior Engineer

(a) The address of the writer, unless the letter is written on company headed paper. There is no punctuation within the address.

(b) The date, with the month written as a word. The most common form of date is '7 May 2004'. This is often put at the left-hand side of the page at this level.

(c) The name and address of the recipient. This may take the form of status and address ('The General Manager, Bridgeco Engineering Co. Ltd'), although if possible the individual's name should also be used. Sometimes 'Dear Sir' or 'Dear Madam' may be used, with an extra line, 'For the attention of...'. If a name is included, it should include an initial ('Ms J Twigg'). Again, there is no punctuation within the name or address.

(d) The greeting: 'Dear...' as appropriate. No initial is used at this point ('Dear Ms Twigg'), and the name is not followed by a comma.

(e) A heading, which identifies the subject of the letter. This may, for instance, be an order number or the name of a project or the same heading as in the letter replied to. The use of a heading enables the writer to begin the text directly, with the first factual information. It is also helpful to the reader, allowing the subject to be identified at once. Sometimes the heading is prefaced by 're:' ('with reference to'), but this is becoming old-fashioned.

(f) Represents the beginning of the text, which contains normal punctuation. Paragraphs are 'blocked' to the left-hand margin rather than indented, and double spacing is left between paragraphs.

(g) The 'courtesy close' sentence, which often causes the writer more difficulty than the rest of the letter. It must be a grammatical sentence (see p. 23), which rules out 'Looking forward to receiving your comments' or 'Thanking you in anticipation', which contain no verb. The phrase 'in anticipation' used in this way should always be avoided: it is a particularly nasty piece of jargon. The nature of the letter will dictate an appropriate, short courtesy close, but 'I look forward to hearing from you', 'Thank you for your cooperation' or 'If I can be of further assistance, please contact me' are all regularly used and satisfactory.

(h) The conclusion: 'Yours...'. Convention dictates that 'Dear Sir', 'Dear Madam' or any form of greeting which does not include the recipient's personal name will be followed by 'Yours faithfully' (capital Y, small f, with no punctuation), to which there is no alternative. As soon as a personal name is involved ('Dear Mr Twigg', or 'Dear Jim'), the most common conclusion is 'Yours sincerely' (capital Y, small s) or, although it is perhaps seen as old-fashioned, 'Yours truly'. Occasionally, if writer and reader are well known to one another, the conclusion can be expanded a little:

Kind regards.

Yours

Jim

This is acceptable as long as it is felt by both parties to be appropriate.

(i) The signature of the writer, or sometimes of someone signing on the writer's behalf.

(j) The typed name, including any relevant titles, such as 'Dr', which should never be added to the signature.

Style

The language in which a letter is written should be as simple as possible, unambiguous and courteous. If it is a reply, it is sensible to begin, 'Thank you for your letter of 6 July'. This is much better than 'I have received your letter of 6 July' (how else could you be replying to it?) or 'I am writing in reply to your letter' (obviously you're writing!), and more grammatical than 'With reference to your letter of 6 July.', which is not a sentence. The recommended version also avoids 'I' as the first word of the letter, which can sound a bit self-important; whenever possible, start with 'you' rather than 'I'. For example:

I know that you are anxious that the completion date is as early as possible

would be better as

You are naturally anxious that . . .

Companies vary in their policy about 'I', 'we' or the impersonal form ('It is agreed that . . .'). Such policy should, of course, be followed. When a choice is available, it is worth noting that 'we' (that is, the writer on behalf of the organisation) is easier to use than the impersonal; it is more concise and sounds more cooperative. 'We agree that' gives a sense of personal concern which is missing from 'It is agreed that'. 'I' may be allowed, but should be reserved for personal involvement; when the writer means '*I* will be at the next meeting of the institution and will be able to discuss the matter with you then', the use of 'we' would be silly. Letter writers are oddly unwilling to refer to themselves directly as 'me', and manage to sound pompous in avoiding it. 'The undersigned', 'the present writer' or even 'myself' distance writer from reader; if writers mean 'please contact me', they should say so.

Above all, letters should be helpful. They go as ambassadors of the writer's company, and if they are overformal, ambiguous in content, wordy or chilling in tone, goodwill is strained. The writer should always be aware of the need to give clear information, offer assistance, sound concerned or offer apologies, as required, and check that the document says exactly what it was meant to say.

Far too often, letters (and reports and other company documentation) are not checked. If they are dictated into a machine and then typed when the originator is far away, there is a special danger that the wrong information is given. Somebody must be responsible for checking that the typed version is correct and attractively set out. If the writer is available, he or she should check the document carefully, as signing it is an acceptance of responsibility for any mistakes it may contain (see also Chapter 6).

▶ Letters are always, and faxes are often, formal documents which represent the company that sends them

---

Activity 4.2 Covering letter and short report

The following information is a discussion of tests carried out on a swaged tube as part of a proposed jointing system. While the technical content is complete, the lack of organisation and paragraphing makes it difficult to read. If this information is to be conveyed to a client outside the writer's organisation, a decision about the most appropriate format has to be made. There is clearly too much detail for a telephone call, although the main result might initially be conveyed that way. A letter is a possibility, although again the amount of technical content would make it unwieldy. The most appropriate choice is a one-page report with a short covering letter. Both documents might be sent by email (with the report as an attachment), although a copy would almost certainly follow by post.

Reorganise and rewrite the information as a report with a covering letter.

On 27 May, Richard MacNamara and I (Sarah Watson) performed a simple test on the 76 mm diameter swaged tube you supplied. We had made first a plaster cast of the inside of the tube and secondly a steel plug to match the cast. The plug was then forced through the tube held by a plate welded around the edge in a compression testing machine. The effect on the swaged end was then similar to that intended for the pull-out test being planned. The tube failed at a load of 218 kN by the cracking of the longitudinal weld (which had been ground flat on the inside previously) after very little distortion. This result would appear to confirm a difficulty with the jointing system being proposed, as suggested previously, and it is not clear what simple steps can be taken to overcome it. The failure load of 218 kN gives a factor of safety of only 1.3 over the normal working load of 168 kN in axial tension. To confirm this figure of 218 kN I suggest that several more specimens are tested in the same way, but it would seem prudent to give consideration to the weld strength problem before embarking on a more expensive series of pull-out tests. 826M40 (EN26) steel will be needed because it has been suggested that failure might require the swaging load of over 600 kN and because the fittings have been designed to be suitable for the thickest available tubes of 168 mm outside diameter (10 mm wall). However, the result of the preliminary test performed last week might indicate that a lower grade material would be suitable. Use of mild steel would save on the cost. As I have suggested, I think we should perform a few more simple push-out tests before going ahead with the pull-out ones.

▶ Reports

Reports, like letters, are written for their readers. This obvious fact is overlooked at the report writer's peril. Most reports convey information about a given subject, such as a project, an accident, tests on equipment or a visit. Many reports are also requests: the writer wants more time, more money or more cooperation to sell a product or an idea. Both formal language and logically presented format must work to the benefit of the reader, who is the most important person. They will then also result in the 'right' response from the point of view of the writer.

Objectives
The reader(s) and the objectives must both be clearly identified at the start of the report writing process. There may be one known reader, or several, or the report might be destined for a wide readership, but the writer needs, as far as possible, to identify who these people are, what their level of technical knowledge is and why they need the report. This will help in the choice of the correct language, that is, the appropriate level of

technicality, with explanation and backup as required. Far too often reports, like letters, use pompous words ('initiate' rather than 'start') and inexact expressions ('in due course', 'regularly'). As in all technical writing, the English language should be used in a formal but flowing and readable way, and as precisely as possible. Technical language should be chosen for the reader and the subject matter, preferably in that order.

The purpose of the report, its objectives, should also be well defined in the writer's mind. The writer will have his or her own reasons for writing the report, perhaps one that is immediate ('I want them to make this decision') and others that are more long term ('I need their cooperation for future projects, even if they reject my suggestions this time'). The reader will also have objectives, and again they may be both short term ('I need advice about making the right decision') and long term ('I wonder if we could ask this writer to cooperate with our next project?').

Identifying the objectives allows the writer to check that all the information given is relevant to the subject and builds up a clear, uncluttered picture of the situation and what should be done about it. This clarification also helps to make the writing concise; report readers are usually busy people who prefer a short document to a long one. There is a tendency among engineers to ramble, often repeating the same information several times, introducing unnecessary details or wandering away from the point.

Structure

Although some reports are read in order from start to finish, far more reports are *used*, with the reader picking and choosing sections which are helpful, of particular interest or needed urgently. The structure of the whole document must be apparent from the contents list, although convention is also a useful guide. A report on a technical process might follow a standard format such as the following:

Title page
Contents page
Summary   (including, very briefly, the main conclusions and recommendations)
Introduction   (with the reason for the investigation, and any constraints in carrying out the work)
Procedure   (how the investigation was carried out)
Results   (the facts which emerged from the investigation)
Discussion   (the implications of the results)
Conclusions   (what is or is not satisfactory)
Recommendations (what should be done as a result of the conclusions)

A long advisory report might have even more sections:

Title page
Acknowledgements
Summary   (including the main conclusions and
                              recommendations)
Contents list   (section numbers, headings and subheadings,
                              page numbers)
Introduction   (putting the reader in the picture, including any
                              necessary background)
Findings   (what was discovered as a result of the work, in
                              numbered sections)
Conclusions   (the implications of what was discovered)
Recommendations   (what should be done in the future)
References   (books, articles etc referred to in the text)
Bibliography   (other related reading)
Appendix (appendices)   (supplementary material)
Annexe (annexes)   (documents bound at the end of the report for
                              the convenience of readers)

The format shown above is complex, much too long for many reports, but the pattern is useful: introduction, factual content, comment or conclusions and, if they are asked for, recommendations. This ordering of information can be followed even if the report is a short one.

Within the given format, reports are closely structured in sections with numbered headings. A short report might need only a small number of headings and in this case there may be no advantage in numbering them. Most reports, and certainly any which are more than a couple of pages in length, have headings numbered for ease of identification and reference. There are various numbering systems, some of them very simple:

1. Background
2. Investigation
3. Comments

Longer reports need a more complex structure, either paragraph numbering or, preferably, decimal notation, in which all headings are numbered, irrespective of the number of paragraphs in the section. This is a clear hierarchical structure, in which sections with major headings can be subdivided into subsections with lesser headings, as follows:

1   MAIN HEADING

1.1   **Subordinate Heading**

1.1.1 Smaller heading

The pattern is repeated, so that:

- sections 2, 3, 4 etc are equal in importance to section 1
- sections 1.2, 6.4, 9.5 etc are equal in importance to section 1.1
- sections 1.1.2, 1.2.6, 8.11.3 etc are equal in importance to section 1.1.1

If the report is very long, a fourth layer, 1.1.1.1 etc can be added, but the numbering should not be extended beyond that.

This numbering system is useful in that it is widely used and recognised, easy to check and logical. Sections can be readily identified: section 2.4 begins with that number and continues to 2.5, and all material in between is subordinate to the 2.4 heading. In this system, all numbers have headings and vice versa, with one exception. Lists are kept clear of the main decimal notation system. Items are identified by single arabic numbers in parentheses to the left of the text, as in the example below:

Headings in reports should be:

1. short, usually not more than five or six words
2. as specific as possible
3. set out in a form appropriate to the numbering hierarchy.

This last point is particularly helpful to readers. If major headings look as if they are major headings (for instance, in bold upper case) and subordinate headings can be identified by their format (for instance, a smaller upper case bold, or lower case bold) as well as by their number, the reader can see the structure of any page of the document immediately. The format of the headings and the numbering system reinforce each other.

▶ Reports have a logical structure which should be clear to the reader; their language is always formal

Dates in reports

All reports should be dated, not least to protect the writer, who is responsible for the accuracy of the information at the time of writing but who cannot be expected to foresee economic or legal changes which could invalidate the conclusions. A visit report is likely to have two dates, that of the visit and that of the writing of the report. If a report is updated and reissued, both dates need to be shown; many company reports have all their textual history, including amendments and updating, shown on the pages immediately after the title page.

Ideally, a report is a document for *use*, planned and written for the convenience of the reader, and structured so that its logic is immediately apparent. The reader should be able to identify and use detailed information without having to work through long paragraphs or pages of text. For this to happen, all the headings must be set out in order on the contents page, together with details of any appendices or annexed material. Readers then have a logical overview of the structure of the document, and can select any section or subsection which they need, seeing how it fits into the report as a whole.

Running headers and footers are also helpful in guiding users through the document. Pagination can be of the '1, 2, 3' variety, or '1 of 6, 2 of 6, 3 of 6' form, which is particularly useful if the pages are looseleaf rather than bound. The numbers are easiest to see and use if they are placed at the top right-hand corner of the page rather than at the bottom. Date, classification and, in a long report, section number can be added to the footer, as can the author's name and title, as long as the latter is short enough not to require an extra line of print.

Most useful of all is the inclusion of a summary at the beginning of the text, unless the material of the report makes a summary impossible (for instance if the purpose of the report is simply to give detailed information to readers, with no suggestion for action).

Summaries in reports

In many reports, the summary is the most important and influential part of the text. As has been suggested above (see p. 72), it has to be placed at the start, perhaps before the contents list and certainly before the introduction, because readers will turn to it before they begin to read any other part of the text. The summary gives a brief resumé of the whole report, emphasising those aspects which are likely to be of most importance to readers, almost always the conclusions and recommendations. In about a third to half a page (the summary would be longer than this only if the report itself were long, perhaps more than 30–40 pages), the writer has to give readers an accurate and unbiased picture of the message contained in the report. Readers will then read this first, go back to it as a reminder of the content, study it to help them to understand technically complex information, and, in some cases, read the summary and nothing more. This is true especially of two categories of readers: managers who are not directly concerned with the work discussed but who need a general view of what is happening, and senior staff who are unlikely to give the time to a full reading of the report but who may well be involved in making decisions on the basis of its recommendations. If they read a clear, well-balanced summary, they are almost inevitably on the side of the writer. Needless to say, the summary is thus highly influential and also difficult to write well. The time needed to produce a good summary should never be underestimated.

▶ The summary is often the most influential part of a report

Summaries are sometimes referred to as 'executive summaries', although strictly speaking these are different: they are longer than a true summary, perhaps several pages in length, and obviously contain more information. They are difficult to produce and often lack the balance of the short summary, including more detail in some areas and less in others. Unless there is a particular reason to include such a summary, it is better avoided. However, the term 'executive summary' is frequently no more than a rather grand title for an ordinary short summary.

Diagrams

Diagrams will often be included, either in the main body of the report or at the end, as appropriate, although in this, as in all decisions, the convenience of the reader must be considered. Generally, it is easier to follow the flow of information if the diagrams are placed near the words that explain them, unless the diagram is so large or lengthy that it would seriously interrupt the reading or it is of interest to only a minority of readers. A detailed circuit diagram, pages of computer code or a table which covers several pages are likely to be too long or too complex for the body of the report, and would almost certainly be better at the end.

A diagram is useful to make an immediate visual impact, often to allow readers to assimilate information that it would be difficult or even impossible to present in words. It must therefore be clear in every detail. This means that it must be large enough for every letter or number to be instantly recognisable (5, 6 and 8, for example, are easily confused if they are printed in too small a font). Space should be used helpfully: in a table, space is often better than grid lines, which can have a dazzling effect; if items on a long vertical axis are grouped in fours or fives with a blank line between groups, the figures will be easier to read than if they are all equally spaced. In producing a great many tabulated figures, the writer should consider how to help different types of reader: sometimes, a graph showing a trend will be appropriate in the body of the report, while detailed figures to several decimal places might be better in an appendix. Knowledge of the reader's needs is, as usual, the best guide.

Within a diagram, all labelling should be placed horizontally, even if the illustration itself is presented in landscape form, that is, if the page has to be rotated 90° in a clockwise direction. Abbreviations, symbols and so on should of course conform to international standards in diagrams as in the text itself.

Clarity is a special consideration in the choice of colour. Generally, dark colours stand out well on white or lightly coloured backgrounds, but if there is writing on top of colour, the contrast must be sufficiently strong for the reader to see the words easily. Black print on a deep red or dark green background will be hard to read, and this is not the only problem presented by these two colours: many men are colour-blind, especially where red and green are concerned, and if these apparently brightly visible colours are used together, for instance to show lines on a graph, many male readers (and an extremely small number of female readers) will be unable to distinguish between them.

It is especially worth checking the clarity of diagrams imported from another source. Definition can sometimes be lost in the transfer, especially if the diagram has to be resized for its new home. Headings in tables can also be moved, so that they no longer clearly belong to the correct column of figures.

Every diagram needs to be identified by a number and a short title. This information is usually placed directly beneath the diagram, along with details of the source or a key if appropriate. The convention for numbering diagrams in reports is that two numbers are used, the first being that of the main section of the report and the second being sequential. Figure 2.2 is therefore the second diagram in section 2 of the report (only the main section numbers are shown, so that this number would be used even if the diagram appeared in section 2.4.1 of the document). Readers need to be told when to look at a diagram. In the appropriate place, a reference (see Figure 2.2) indicates that the reader will be helped by the diagram at this point of the text.

Activity 4.3 Long report

The information that follows comes from a real-life technical report, but the structure has been removed so that it reads as an essay, with paragraphs but without numbered headings. It is difficult to extract details from so many words and figures,

(Cont'd)

and an engineer attempting to use the information would find it frustrating and no doubt extremely irritating.
Organise this material into a well-structured report that could be used easily and accurately.

The effect of acoustic ceiling tiles on noise at the County Swimming Pools, Northwich. February 2003.

After acoustic tiles had been installed in the ceiling of the Learner Pool at the County Swimming Pools, Northwich, Jim Downs, a member of the Parks and Leisure Subcommittee, was asked to liaise with Dr Andrew Poynter, Senior Lecturer in the Department of Mechanical Engineering at the local University of Abimouth, in order to investigate the effect of the tiles on noise levels.

Andrew Poynter had been involved in 2001 in testing noise levels at the Pool, after staff and parents had complained to the Council. At that time, he had recommended that the Council install acoustic tiles manufactured by Fraser and Macfarlane to an area of 114 m². He measured current reverberation times (see Table 1) and also noise levels. These latter were recorded as an average of 92 dBA, with a maximum of 103 dBA and a minimum of 87 dBA.

The Council approved Andrew Poynter's recommendation, especially as both he and the tile manufacturer's representative predicted shorter reverberation times (see Table 1) and lower noise levels if the tiles were fitted. The new acoustic ceiling was therefore installed in November 2002.

Two months later, Dr Poynter was asked to assess the effect of the ceiling, and to give Jim Downs a report on the findings. He agreed to do this. On 1 February 2003, they visited the Learner Pool together when there was the usual weekend attendance of about 35 people, adults and children. This was approximately the same number as in 2001 when the original tests were carried out.

Andrew Poynter found that an area of 180 m² had in fact been treated with the acoustic tiles, but he did not consider that this invalidated his original predictions, although of course the figures were no longer precise.

The backing of the tiles was fibre glass in film bags, which was also different from that used in the earlier tests. This backing could have been responsible for the beneficial results that were obtained.

The reverberation times were measured and compared with the times predicted by Andrew Poynter and by the representative of Fraser and Macfarlane. They were found to be much shorter (see Table 1). Noise levels were also tested, with the average now 77 dBA, the maximum being 87 dBA and the minimum 71 dBA. This was a pleasing decrease over the earlier level.

Dr Poynter also talked to the staff at the Learner Pool. The instructors and the pool attendants all agreed that the general noise level had gone down, which made their working conditions pleasanter. They also felt that the intelligibility of speech had been greatly improved, so that they could now both hear more clearly and identify who was making a particular noise. This was obviously good from a safety point of view, and made the training of youngsters easier. They declared themselves to be delighted with the new ceiling.

After he had completed his assessment, Andrew Poynter reported that he was so pleased with the results that he felt the Council should extend the acoustic ceiling. The general noise level had clearly fallen and the reverberation times were much shorter, probably as a result of the backing of the tiles. The same kind of tiles should obviously be used in the future. The staff felt that their work had become easier and the safety level had improved, which must be good for everyone.

Andrew Poynter prepared his report along these lines and presented it to Jim Downs for consideration by the Council.

Table 1 below shows the measurements of reverberation times.

Table 1 Reverberation times in the Learner Pool (curtain open)

Frequency (Hz)	2001 (seconds)	A. Poynter's recommendation (seconds)	Fraser & Mcfarlane's prediction* (seconds)	2003 (seconds)
125	1.75	–	2.8	0.7
250	2.2	–	2.0	0.4
500	2.4	1.5	1.3	0.55
1000	3.8	1.65	1.5	0.8

(Cont'd)

Table 1 (Continued)				
Frequency (Hz)	2001 (seconds)	A. Poynter's recommendation (seconds)	Fraser & Mcfarlane's prediction* (seconds)	2003 (seconds)
2000	3.6	1.65	1.7	0.85
4000	3.0	1.5	1.6	0.9
8000	–	–	–	0.55

*Fraser & Macfarlane's prediction was based upon $114\,m^2$ of treatment whereas the actual area installed was $180\,m^2$.

▶ Specifications and instructions

Specifications are perhaps halfway between reports and procedures: they present the standard expected or against which the work can be tested, and for this reason often incorporate or are closely linked to British or international standards. Specifications may show, for example, how machinery is to be manufactured or maintained, or how a system is to be designed or operated, and the language in which they are written must conform to specific rules. Procedures are of two sorts: *general* procedures, which indicate that the work should be done in a particular way, and *specific* procedures, which give precise instructions for carrying it out. Instructions themselves simply tell the user what to do, often with little elaboration, although explanatory notes or diagrams are sometimes included.

Style and language

In all these forms of instruction writing, a major source of difficulty is the use of a group of words which are often confused: *can/could, may/might, should/would, will/shall/must*. They are defined as follows:

- *Can/could* are used to show ability:

    The car can reach 110 mph.
    It could travel even faster in different road conditions.

- *May/might* show permission or possibility:

    The car may (is allowed to) travel at 70 mph on the motorway.

The lorry might arrive (there is the possibility that it will) before dark if it is not held up by a traffic jam.

- *Might* can also be used negatively:

  The lorry might have arrived if the road had not been flooded.

- *Able* means skilled or equipped to perform a specified job; it has no suggestion of willingness or intention:

  The engineer is able to repair the damage. (He or she is capable of repairing the damage.)

- *Should/would* are nowadays used interchangeably, and their force is often ambiguous, as in the following examples:

  I wonder if I should drive so fast. ('should' implies hesitation, whether I ought to or not)
  I should go as quickly as possible. ('should' implies moral imperative, under an obligation to)
  He would go if conditions were right. ('would' implies unlikely possibility, conditions are not right)
  He would go in spite of our warnings. ('would' implies determination, he insisted on going)

As a result of this confusion, the choice between 'should' and 'would' is often one of sound, as at the beginning of letters:

  I should be grateful if you would kindly supply the following.

'Will' is also ambiguous in writing, although in speech it is often made clear by emphasis, as in the following examples:

  I will mend the car tomorrow. ('will' implies future action)
  I will mend the car tomorrow in spite of my other commitments. ('will' implies determination)
  The garage will be responsible for those repairs that are covered by the guarantee. ('will' implies future obligation)

All the above examples suggest the difficulty of using 'should', 'would', or 'will' casually in technical writing. However, there is one very strong convention: 'shall' is generally used to express obligation, and is now so forceful that, particularly in specifications, it has become an instruction word:

> The company shall be liable for the cost of maintaining the equipment.
> The engineer shall carry out the repairs as agreed.

In the writing of **specifications**, 'shall' should be used as the normal word to represent obligation: the company is deemed to be liable, the engineer will have to carry out the repairs. In other contexts, there is not the same degree of uniformity, and the writer should remember that 'shall' can be interpreted as a simple future:

> I shall go to enquire about the order tomorrow or the following day.

It must therefore be made clear in such documents if the word is used to convey an obligation; in a specification, this would be taken for granted.

The other word which is available to writers of specifications is *must*, which allows no option, and which carries an extra layer of meaning: it tells the user that the obligation is not simply that of the current document. The action is mandatory because of 'higher' authority, for instance because the law demands it. This distinction between 'shall' and 'must' is a useful one, and should be maintained, not least because it is widely recognised.

For this reason, it is better in specification writing to avoid less precise expressions such as 'is to/are to/has to'. In everyday life, we use them to suggest obligation, but in a technical document they can cause uncertainty: if this action *shall* be done and that one *has to* be done, are there different levels of obligation, and if so, which is the stronger? There is, of course, no recognised answer to this.

A good writing style is always appreciated by readers, but in the case of specifications it must, if necessary, be sacrificed to accuracy. Many sentences will sound repetitive, especially in the constant use of 'shall', but this is in the nature of specifications and cannot be avoided. A 'literary', flowing style is almost impossible to achieve in any kind of instructional writing: sentences within a passage tend to be too often of the same length and structure.

Specification writers sometimes fall into the trap of using pseudo-legal language such as 'aforesaid' or 'always provided that'; this sounds pompous and should be avoided, as should a combination of words that mean the same, such as 'orders, instructions and directions'. Words need always to be chosen carefully, with the needs of the specification user in mind. Terms such as 'regularly' or 'workmanlike' sound helpful, but how regular is regular? Once every century? 'Workmanlike' implies that all workmen operate in the same way and to the same standard, which is not, alas, the case.

Most companies nowadays have written **procedures** which are regularly appraised and updated, and here too there is a recognised terminology.

A general procedure describes how actions should be taken (it does not give instructions) and the word 'should' is used, exactly as it was earlier in this sentence. Specific procedures, however, are much more like **work instructions**, and may be written either in specification terms ('shall' and 'must') or in the usual language of direct instructions, using the imperative form of the verb. This is the 'command' form, 'do this', as in the following examples:

> Check the equipment before signing the form.
> Inform the safety officer immediately if the machine is to be moved.
> Replace the guard on the machine immediately after maintenance.

In these sentences, the verbs 'check', 'inform' and 'replace' have the force of a command; there is no possibility of misunderstanding the intention.

The engineer, in preparing **instructions**, is not in the business of asking, suggesting, recommending or preferring. Orders have to be carried out exactly, and the only safe way of writing is to make each step sound like an order. We are not asked if we would mind not smoking as we take petrol at the service station: the results would be too awful if we decided not to comply. Nevertheless, it is sensible to give a reason for the order unless it is equally obvious. 'No unauthorised entry', for instance, might be followed by the familiar radioactivity symbol to warn us of the hazard.

British and International Standards combine to make many hazard warnings international in use, and the colour codes (red for prohibition, yellow for caution, blue for mandatory actions and green for safe conditions) should, of course, be adhered to. Words and symbols are both used in warning notices, and a combination is often sensible (for example, the 'no smoking' sign is often accompanied by a crossed-out cigarette).

Instructions which are also warnings should be written in a positive rather than a negative form if at all possible:

> Do not leave equipment switched on.

is better as:

> Switch off equipment.

Some instructions, however, are negative in themselves, even doubly negative, as in:

> Unauthorised persons may not change grinding wheels.

If possible, this should be made positive, as in:

> Grinding wheels should be changed ONLY by authorised persons

Both style and layout are important considerations in the preparation of instructions, as they are in any technical writing. It is easy to see why. Instructions have to be carried out; they must be unambiguous or the wrong action will be taken, and they must be well set out or actions may be omitted or performed in the wrong order.

The correct choice of words is essential throughout the document. The writer must select words not only for their accuracy but also for the reader's understanding. Instructions are usually written for people junior to the writer in status, knowledge and experience: the difficulty is to think oneself back into the position of the reader and write accordingly.

Imagination is needed to recreate the reader's lack of knowledge and also to envisage the reader's physical position. Words such as *left, right, back* and *front* depend on point of view. Similarly, words such as *near, far, close, beside, behind*, and even *big* and *small*, are subjective. Precise information is needed. Other words create problems: *appropriate, relative, substantial* and *suitable* all depend on the reader's perception, and should be clarified or avoided.

▶ Structure and layout

All types of instructional writing have their conventions. In the case of **specifications**, the format is rather like that of a report, although there are a few differences that need to be highlighted. A common format for a specification is as follows:

Title page
Contents list
Introduction (the first numbered section)
Scope (range and depth of coverage; limitations if appropriate)
References (normative and informative – see below)
Definitions (of specified terms – see below)
Glossary (abbreviations, etc)
Main text of the specification, in appropriate sections
Appendices (additional information for particular readers)

Two of these sections need extra comment. Specifications contain two types of reference: normative and informative. Normative references cross-refer to other specifications which are to be used alongside the one in which the reference appears. It may be necessary to show which has priority, for instance, by adding 'in case of conflict, this Specification takes precedence over BS...'. Informative references are similar to those found in reports, giving details of other publications which have been quoted or are useful for further guidance.

Some names or terms have a specific meaning throughout the document, and by convention these have initial capital letters. So the word 'Client' may have a capital C to show that the word stands for the particular Client for whom the document is being prepared. 'Works' or 'Contractor' may similarly have the initial capital. In writing the specification, it is obviously essential to be consistent: 'client' with a small 'c' will be interpreted as any client other than the one for whom the document is intended.

The main body of a specification, like that of a report, will have numbered sections, as in:

2 MATERIALS
2.1 Cement
2.2 Aggregates
2.3 Admixtures

and so on; there are likely to be far more divisions than in a report, and the specifier might need five or six decimal places and perhaps even **a**, **b** and **c** after that.

The organisation and layout of **instructions** are also important. The most important rule is: one step at a time in a logical order. Each step should be numbered, and sequential arabic numbers are the easiest to follow. Numbering identifies clearly the individual stages to be completed, and is a useful reference tool if the process is interrupted (each step can be ticked off as it is finished).

The writer is also helped by a numbered sequence as it helps in checking that all stages have been included in the correct order, that is, the order in which the reader will carry them out. Never backtrack in instruction writing: imagine being told that the battery must be checked after all naked flames have been extinguished. The *first* action (extinguishing all naked flames) must come before the *second* action (checking the battery).

Space is an important tool, to limit the amount of information which the reader has to take in at one time. Space should be left between heading(s) and instructions, and each instruction should begin on a new line. General comments, such as 'This procedure should be carried out weekly', should be either at the beginning or at the end, but clearly separated from the instructions themselves. If additional information is needed within the text, it should be distinguished either by position (for instance in a margin to the right of the instructions) or by font (for instance by being in italics). Warnings must be especially clear, and if possible placed both at the beginning and at the appropriate stage of the instructions. Attention should be drawn to them, by the use of red and (not least because colour-blindness is common) capital letters, underlining or some other identifying mark.

Sometimes instructions can be grouped, with extra space at the end of each sequence and appropriate headings. Whatever form is chosen, the pattern of instructions should be clear to users, to increase their efficiency and give them confidence that they are doing the job correctly.

▶ Instructions must be appropriate in content and language, and set out in a way which helps the user

---

Activity 4.4 Instructions

The following set of instructions for the design of a state machine is written in a rambling and imprecise way. Reorganise and rewrite it to make it easier to use.

First of all, you should make a statement defining the state machine in terms of a state diagram and then after the number of required state variables has been determined and the state representations chosen, you can determine both the next-state functions of the present state and inputs and the output functions of the present state and inputs.

▶ Summary

- ▶ Paragraphs have unity of theme
- ▶ Good paragraphing produces space on the page and encourages the reader
- ▶ List information whenever it is possible to do so
- ▶ Set out numbers in a way which is easy to use
- ▶ Use a conventional format with which the reader is familiar
- ▶ Emails are not conversational; they can be printed out and turned into documents
- ▶ Letters are always, and faxes are often, formal documents which represent the company that sends them

▶ Reports have a logical structure which should be clear to the reader; their language is always formal
▶ The summary is often the most influential part of a report
▶ Instructions must be appropriate in content and language, and set out in a way which helps the user

5 Good style

▶ Definition of good style

Good style can roughly be defined as style which is appropriate to the needs of the reader. A particular piece of information might, for example, be presented as original research in the publication following an academic conference. Subsequently, it might appear in a textbook for under-graduates; it might become such a basic contribution to knowledge of the subject that it would appear in a newspaper article for the intelligent but non-specialist reader; it might be published in school textbooks; eventually, it might be found in a children's encyclopaedia. In each manifestation, the information will be presented with vocabulary, sentence structure, explanation and examples suited to the current readership. If the level is estimated incorrectly, the information will not be accepted. It will be seen as 'too difficult', 'bewildering' or 'condescending', and will be rejected by the reader for whom it was intended.

Such extreme variations of readership are unusual, but they illustrate the need to write in a style which is helpful and encouraging to the reader. Writing in a vacuum, for the sake of writing rather than for a clearly defined audience, is unlikely to result in good style, and, indeed, the end product will probably not be read at all. The first requirement of good writing is that it suits the reader.

▶ Good style is appropriate to the needs of the reader

Earlier in this book, we considered choice of words, organisation of sentences and paragraphs, and appropriate format. In doing so, considerations of style were important. Sentence length, for example, can help or hinder reading: very long sentences are nearly always difficult to read. They may have their place in works of literature, but not in the immediate transmission of engineering information. However, good style is more than the correct choice of words or appropriate length of sentences. It also involves a wise choice of material and the appropriate putting together of discrete pieces of information. Both aspects will be considered in this chapter.

▶ Readership and objectives

Long before the first word of a technical paper or report is written, the prospective writer needs to ask and answer a series of questions:

- Who is my reader/are my readers?
- How much does the reader know about this subject?
- What is the reader's experience of this type of work?

The reader or readers must first be identified so that the writer can choose the style correctly. How technical should the vocabulary be? How many terms will need explanation and how much can the writer take for granted? What kind of examples will be helpful?

It will not always be possible to find exact answers to these questions. The initial readers might pass on the document to other people about whom the writer knows nothing; a report, for instance, might be read again years after its first distribution because a similar problem has arisen.

Nevertheless, the writer needs to attempt to find answers, and assess how far such questions can be answered under current circumstances.

Next, the writer moves on to objectives, both his or her own, in writing the document, and the reader's, in sparing the time to read it. Again, there is a useful series of questions:

- Why should a busy writer find it necessary to commit this information to a written form?
- Why should the reader, busily involved with other work, bother to read this document?
- What does the writer want to happen as a result of writing this document?
- What does the reader want to happen as a result of reading this document?

One clear result of asking these questions is that the writer will recognise the need for brevity. Both writer and reader are busy engineers with other preoccupations than the paper in question, and they will be helped if it is as short as possible. Part of the courtesy of good style is to avoid wasting the reader's time with what is unnecessary or irrelevant.

These final questions, about objectives, need more careful analysis. What does the writer hope to achieve? The answer may seem obvious: she wants her new young assistant to be able to carry out instructions competently and in safety; he wants the answer to his letter to be an order for his company's product; they (much technical writing is the output of a group rather than an individual) want their report to result in the company installing the most appropriate system. There are, however, other hidden motives: to persuade the client to think well of the company, encourage superiors to think well of the writer or further a promising career.

If the writer is to be successful in such objectives, the information must not only be presented briefly. It must also be accurate and clear to the reader. Chapter 7 will look at accuracy of presentation, but good style involves choosing words and examples which convey precisely what the writer means, and which will be understood by the reader in the same way. Ambiguity or careless use of words will blur the issue and may produce the wrong result. Good writing demands precision of thought and precision of language.

▶ Good style has its ABC: accuracy, brevity, clarity

The 'courtesy' of good style was mentioned above. Courtesy involves consideration for the reader, which may for instance dictate the way in which he or she is addressed. 'He or she' is used advisedly; some engineering documents still assume that the readership is male. In letters especially, the address should be correct (see p. 66 for a more detailed discussion of this point), but in longer documents, the writer may feel that a decision has to be made. 'He or she' used repeatedly is cumbersome and long-winded; the decision made in writing this book was to avoid prejudiced language (often by the use of the plural), and keep the use of 'he or she' to a minimum.

▶ Formality

Courtesy will also be a factor in decisions about formality. On the whole, emails are informal, faxes may be formal or informal (see pp. 64–5) letters are more formal, and reports and technical papers are very formal, although there are exceptions in each case. Instructions are impersonal (not 'You must switch off the engine' but 'switch off the engine'). Formal writing does not allow the use of abbreviations such as 'it's' or 'can't', or the inclusion of slang or casual expressions better suited to the spoken language. In the most formal writing, the reader is not addressed directly ('You will find that' becomes 'It will be found that'), and abbreviations such as 'eg' or 'ie' are often written out in full, especially in passages of continuous prose.

Sometimes company policy dictates the level of formality, but if the engineer has to make the decision, it will be based on a consideration of the company's relationship to the reader and also on the information itself. If a full report format is chosen, the style must be formal, although a very short report for the use of colleagues might be written in a slightly less formal style. Once the appropriate style is chosen, it must be used consistently; any deviation to a more formal or less formal style will distract the reader and interrupt the flow of the passage.

Activity 5.1 Levels of formality

In the following passage, the writing style varies between the informal, the formal and the pompous. Rewrite the passage, making it consistent in a formal style which would be appropriate in a technical document.

The members of the team have done three experiments so far, but at the end of the day they may not get the results they expect. If the

(Cont'd)

results are inconclusive, they may have to start again from scratch and repeat all the work. It's a pity they didn't bother to take advice from more experienced engineers right back at the inception of the project. Documentation was indisputably available which would have shown the necessity of further preliminary investigation. Could this waste of time have been prevented? It seems probable, if the aforementioned proposal for an initial feasibility study had been implemented at the beginning.

▶ Active and passive

Formality may also dictate whether the writing is active or passive. An active style moves directly from subject to verb to object:

> I recommend this policy.

The use of 'I' is likely to be too informal for company style, or the writer may want to stress that he or she is writing as part of the company, in which case a more suitable form might be:

> We recommend this policy.

However, courtesy or company policy may dictate that the passive is used. The object (policy, in the example given) now becomes the subject, and the person carrying out the action is not mentioned, unless in the cumbersome and unlikely form 'by me'. The sentence will now read:

> This policy is recommended.

The personal 'I' or 'we' has disappeared, and it is no longer clear who has made the recommendation.

Traditionally, formal scientific and technical writing has used the passive, and this is still generally the convention in reports and specifications; in emails or letters it has tended to lose favour as part of a general move towards greater informality, although company policy in letter writing may still dictate a formal style. It is inclined to be long-winded, as in the following example:

> It is recommended that the new staffing levels be applied by each department as soon as possible.

This sentence contains 17 words, while the active form:

> We recommend that each department applies the new staffing levels as soon as possible.

contains only 14. The passive also tends to detract from individual responsibility:

> I recommend ...

is a personal opinion, while

> We recommend ...

is agreed by the company, but

> It is recommended ...

remains unattributable.

In the case of a specification, there is a strong case for using the active form. The allocation of responsibilities is often part of the job of a specifier, and the name or position of the person who has to take a specified action is likely to come at the start of a sentence if the active is used, and at the end of the sentence in the passive. The first few words of any sentence will carry more emphasis than those that follow, and in this way stress is put on the important words that identify the responsible person.

There is one byproduct of the passive which is worth noting. In changing from an active statement to a passive statement, it is easy to give universal significance to what was intended in a more limited way:

> I believe that ...

introduces my own opinion, while

> It is believed that ...

suggests that many other people agree with my belief. Indeed, when

> I cannot accept the idea that ...

becomes

> The idea is unacceptable ...

the world is clearly on our side.

Modern style, then, tends to prefer the active to the passive, but there can be no absolute rule, good style being essentially style which is appropriate to the occasion and the reader.

▶ Use the passive generally in reports, but the active when the identity of the responsible person has to be stressed

---

Activity 5.2 Active and passive

The following passage is written in the passive. Rewrite it in the active form, and then compare the two versions. How have the meaning and emphasis been changed by the use of the active?

The correct running and maintenance of the machine was Jim's responsibility. When it failed to function correctly, there was an investigation by the manager, who found that regular maintenance had not been carried out, but that the records had been completed as if all the requirements had been met. The machine was seen to be functioning at well below capacity, and as the guard had not been positioned correctly, there was a risk to the operative. Jim was reported by a colleague to have been ill at the time.

▶ Signs, symbols and abbreviations

Courtesy to the reader also demands that help be given over those aspects of the document which might cause confusion. Signs, symbols and abbreviations are all potentially ambiguous, and the writer should again ask a series of questions:

- Will I use technical (or other) signs, symbols and abbreviations in my document?
- Can I reasonably expect that the reader will interpret them correctly?
- Is there guidance which I should give, for instance should I quote an appropriate British Standard?
- Would a glossary be helpful to my readers?

Guidance is available to the writer (see Further reading, p. 143), but readers also often need help. As far as abbreviations are concerned, there is a traditional form of explanation. The first time the abbreviation is used, the term is given in full followed by the abbreviation in brackets. Thereafter, the abbreviation can stand alone. This is appropriate for a book or a technical article, but is less useful in a report, which may not be read in order, beginning to end. A glossary, listing all such expressions in alphabetical order, allows the reader to check a meaning from any point in the text. However, if the term is used only once or twice in a lengthy document, it is often easier to write it in full each time rather than make the reader look for an explanation. Glossaries have another advantage: if the reader is familiar with the abbreviation, he or she can ignore the glossary, while other readers can if necessary remind themselves several times of the meaning. Needless to say, the glossary must always be listed on the contents page.

▶ Mathematical material

Measurements and numbering also follow conventions, and it is wise for an engineer to follow British Standards or SI units, or guidance provided by one of the engineering institutions whenever possible. There are sometimes areas of possible confusion caused by common usage, such as *m*, which is the abbreviation for *metre* or *metres*, but not, as it is widely used, for miles.

Arabic numerals should always be used in preference to roman numerals, which can be confused and which in any case are not so easily recognised or understood nowadays. Numbers should also be given in three-digit groups (674 320, with a space rather than the traditional comma to separate thousands from hundreds), and a full stop is the most easily recognisable form of decimal point (as opposed to the comma, widely favoured in the rest of Europe and officially accepted in the UK as an alternative decimal point). Current rules with SI units suggest no space between degrees and temperature scale, for example 30°C, but a space between figures and abbreviations for units of measurement, for example 30 mm.

Small numbers, up to ten, are usually written as words, while larger numbers are given as figures. This convention should be applied with care, as there are various exceptions. Round numbers are always given in words ('about a million miles'). If many large and small numbers are quoted in the same text, it may look better to use figures in every case, including the occasional small number. No sentence should ever begin with a figure: write the number as a word, or, if necessary, change the word order in the sentence. Decisions about the presentation of numbers are best made in the light of the context, with the convenience of the reader uppermost in the mind of the writer.

▶ Follow national, international or professional conventions in presenting signs, symbols, units of measurement and abbreviations

Many forms of writing by engineers include data sets, diagrams representing the data sets and equations; it may also be necessary to describe the mathematical model in use.

Data sets

Most commonly, data sets are in the form of a long list or table of values. In deciding how to present this information, it is essential to assess how it is to be used, both by the reader and by the writer later in the document. Data sets for a series of experiments, for example, may be kept separate or combined; if the writer wants to discuss separate runs of an experiment in the main body of the text, it is essential to present the data for each run separately. As with any diagram, every table of data needs a number and title to identify it and for easy reference.

Sometimes it will be necessary to include both the raw data itself and the charts and diagrams that come from it. As with all technical writing, the convenience of the reader is paramount, and it may be wise, for instance, to introduce the diagram, explaining its purpose, and then present it in the main text, relegating the list of data to an appendix for those readers who need to study it in detail.

Developing a model and presenting equations

Information gleaned from raw data is used to create a mathematical description, such as a set of equations; this is usually referred to as a *model* of the situation(s) under consideration. In describing such a model, the factors that are taken into account must be set out unambiguously, and in writing the equations, it must be clear what each variable represents. Both these criteria may be fulfilled together, as in the following example:

> On the basis of last year's information, we believe that if the price of Toaster A is £x, the profit p we will make by selling n toasters is given by the formula
>
> $p = n \times x \times 0.67$
>
> Note that this model assumes that profit is only a function of price and the number of units sold. Factors such as the availability or price of our competitors' products are not taken into account.

In this example, the variables are defined in the text and there is a clear statement of the limitations of the model. Incidentally, it is also clear what the purpose of the model is: to find the profit to be made in selling toasters!

Using equation editors

Many word-processing packages include an equation editor that allows the presentation of mathematical material. Each has its own peculiarities, and often trial and error is the best way to become familiar with what is available. Perhaps the most important and most common limitation is that while an equation editor may allow the writer to produce an equation that looks perfect, the word processor will treat it as a separate object inserted within the document. This can lead to page set-up problems, such as lines becoming broken in inappropriate places, or even large chunks of equation not appearing in printouts. Wherever possible, check on a printout that equations are displayed accurately; if it is essential to transmit equations electronically, send a hard copy as backup.

In any mathematical context, words such as 'then' and 'therefore' should be used with care. 'Then' can be useful to separate condition from consequence in the context of mathematical notation. 'Therefore' will be used to show a logical connection whatever its context, but a long string of 'therefores' in a mathematical argument is poor style, just as a sequence of 'thens' is clumsy in describing a chain of events (see p. 101).

▶ All tables, charts and diagrams must have numbers and titles for easy reference

▶ When using an equation editor, check accuracy from a printout

▶ Make the purpose of each equation clear and explain what each variable represents

▶ Use of examples

Sometimes the impact of the text is enhanced by the use of an example or a simple analogy which aids the understanding of a difficult idea. There are two rules for using examples: they must be at the correct level for the readership, and they must be widely understood. The writer should not 'overexplain', giving examples when the point is already sufficiently clear. At the same time, an analogy which is woven into the text, as in the following example from the essay of a student engineer, can be helpful to the reader's understanding and also enliven the text, adding a light-hearted touch to a serious subject:

> The problem of progressive collapse can be likened to the toppling of dominoes. As one domino becomes unstable and falls, the impulse that

it implants on its neighbour will cause further destabilisation. This will continue until the entire line of dominoes has collapsed. Stronge (1986) has evaluated the conditions required for the propagation of this wave of destabilisation. Obviously, if the separation, l, of the dominoes is greater than the height, L, the destabilisation of one domino cannot have an effect on the next. Less obvious is the fact that if the dominoes are closely spaced, the wave of collapse will run only for a limited distance before stopping. The spread of the collapse wave is fuelled by the release of potential energy stored in the upright dominoes. If this energy were not available, the process would be arrested by friction. In structures, failures may progress catastrophically, as in the case of Ronan Point, where a single failure spread, domino fashion, throughout the structure.

In this passage, the writer has extended his example beyond the obvious, and has then developed his principal discussion, of progressive collapse in buildings, on the basis, previously established, of the collapse of the dominoes. There is one potential problem. Pleasant though the example is, it will work only if the reader is familiar with dominoes. A writer must always be alert to the danger of examples which seem clear in one cultural context, but which are not helpful to the rest of the world.

▶ A well-chosen example helps the reader's understanding and gives life to the text

▶ References

The passage above illustrates a common form of textual reference to books or articles quoted, that is, the author's name and the date of publication, in brackets (this is known as the Harvard system). An alternative is to use a small superscript number for each reference. Either style is acceptable, although the latter is better avoided in papers which contain mathematical material, as the superscript number is easily confused with, for instance, such numbers in equations. Whichever form of textual mark is chosen, full bibliographical details must always be provided at the end of the document. These include, for books, the name of the author or authors, date, title, publisher, place of publication, edition number (unless it is the first edition) as in the example below:

Fisher, Barry (1995) *How to Document ISO 9000 Quality Systems*, Ramsbury Books, Marlborough

As the book you are now consulting is a third edition, this information needs to be added:

> van Emden, Joan (2005) *Writing for Engineers*, 3rd edn, Palgrave Macmillan, Basingstoke

If there are two authors, both are generally given, but if there are more, the first is given with et al. (and others), as in:

> Bright, K et al. (2004) *Buildings for all to use*, CIRIA Publication c610, CIRIA, London

The appropriate details for articles are author's name, title of article, name of journal, volume number, date and page reference, as follows:

> Green, S D and May, S C (2003) Re-engineering construction: going against the grain, *Building Research and Information*, **31** (2): 97–106

Publications which result from conferences and technical meetings are treated in much the same way, although the place and date of the occasion itself should be included, as in:

> Chaplin, C R (2003) *Rope tension in double drum traction winches*, OIPEEC Technical Meeting, Business School, Lenzburg, Switzerland, September 2003, ed. I M L Ridge, pp. 201–12

The exact format for presenting such information varies, and it is wise to consult the major journals in the writer's own discipline and follow the style which they use. Needless to say, the essential qualities of all references are that they should be accurate and consistent.

▶ References should show full and accurate bibliographical details, and should be consistent in form

Nowadays, there is an extra type of reference for which there is as yet no convention: material from the internet. It is wise to record as much information as possible, including not only the writer (if known) and the title, but also the web address and, most importantly, the date. One of the problems of following up this kind of reference is that the website might have changed or disappeared; if full information is given, writers have done their best to show the source of their material.

Giving the source of information which is not the writer's own is, of course, an essential part of the courtesy of good writing. Plagiarism, copying someone else's work without attributing it to its original author, is both immoral and illegal, and rightly so: academics especially base their careers, and certainly their promotion, on their research and the intellectual property that results from it, and to use such work without giving its source is a form of theft. A reference such as those given above will show the origin of the material in a conventional way, and indicates the honesty of the writer. It is always worth making a record of any material that is to be quoted, or research which is to be mentioned, at the time it is found, as it may otherwise be difficult afterwards to remember where it came from.

▶ A readable style

Engineers who follow all the rules and guidelines for good writing some-times continue to feel that their documents do not flow well. Good style includes a felicity in choice of words and a sense of the rhythm of a passage which come naturally to some writers (of all disciplines) but which are not easily achieved by others. Nevertheless, it is important to be aware of some of the ways in which writing style can be improved, even if a high standard of literature is beyond the reach of the writer. Reading one's own writing out loud and listening critically is a good way to improve style, as awkward repetition, poor sentence structure or abrupt paragraph endings often become obvious as we hear them. For instance, the sentence before last originally ended with 'beyond the writer's reach', but the repeated 'r' sound is ugly, and a simple change to 'beyond the reach of the writer' immediately improved the style. Two more real-life examples from the writing of engineers show how improvements in style can be made.

> The problem was exacerbated by the existence of unclear perceptions by those engineers involved in the project of who the client really was.

If this sentence is read aloud, the awkwardness of the repeated 'by ... of' construction is apparent. There is a secondary repetition of sounds in 'exacerbated' and 'existence', but a much more serious problem results from the use of two heavy abstract words, 'existence' and 'perceptions'. The sentence also ends in a weak style, with a run of short words following the long and complicated words – there is almost a sense of anticlimax – and the meaningless word 'really'.

The first problem to tackle is that of the two abstract words. 'Existence' simply means that something *is*, and 'perceptions' means what they (the engineers) *saw* or *understood*, or, in this case, failed to understand. Once this part of the sentence is simplified (and the long word 'exacerbated' replaced by the simpler 'made worse'), the repetitions will disappear. Out of the mass of words, a simple statement appears:

> The engineers involved in the project were unsure of the client's identity. This made the problem worse.

▶ Avoid abstract words as far as possible. Simple, direct language is almost always easier for the reader

> We would recommend that the complete landlord's sub-mains cabling system is tested with insulation resistance tests results noted for each cable in a schedule with a basic schematic drawing.

If this sentence is read aloud, the problems quickly become clear. Where should the pause come? We might choose to put a comma after 'tested', but there is still the difficulty of 'insulation resistance tests results' – a nasty collection of nouns which fail to form a clear pattern of meaning. 'Test results' seems more natural than 'tests results' even if more than one test is carried out, and the sentence can then be divided into two separate stages: the tests were recommended, and the results should be noted. This suggests two sentences. Other minor improvements can be made, such as 'We recommend' rather than 'We would recommend', which always sounds hesitant and uncertain, and the word 'complete' should presumably refer to the system rather than the landlord! The passage will then read as follows:

> We recommend that the landlord's complete sub-mains cabling system is tested. The results of insulation resistance tests should be noted in a schedule, together with a basic schematic drawing.

This is certainly easier to read and understand.

▶ Listen critically to your own work

▶ Structure and emphasis

Good writing, then, avoids abstraction and is direct and uncomplicated. Since the written word lacks the stress given by the human voice, it has to be clear, logical and precise. It also demands variety. We have probably all read boring passages in which sentences begin 'First, we...' 'Next, we...' 'Then...' 'Then...' and so on. More than two sentences which begin with the same words sound monotonous, as do sentences which have very weak beginnings, such as 'Another example is when...', or 'There are two examples of this and these are...'. A little thought on the part of the writer will usually produce a more interesting and encouraging version of the sentence.

Technical writing can easily become back to front, with the main point following subordinate information so that the reader has to wait to find out what the subject is. An extreme example of this tendency follows:

> Bolted to the stub shaft is the drive gear for the camshaft and bolted to this drive gear is the engine flywheel.

If each part of this sentence is turned round, it will be easier to read:

> The engine flywheel is bolted to the drive gear for the camshaft, which in turn is bolted to the stub shaft.

Generally speaking, it is best to start with the main point of a sentence, not least as it will then get most emphasis; the difference can be seen in the following two sentences:

> It will be the end of the week before the process is complete.

> The process will be complete at the end of the week.

Sometimes a clue about the correct ordering of information is given by a key word such as 'urgent', 'essential' or 'dangerous'. Such words should always come near the start of the sentence or their impact is diminished, as in this real-life example:

> Due to the lack of resources, corners could and would be cut and this would result in dangerous practices being carried out.

There are two clues to the weakness of this: 'due to' at the beginning of a sentence nearly always means that the information is not well structured, and the word 'dangerous' is too strong to be hidden two-thirds of the way through the sentence. A short, well-ordered version makes more impact:

> Dangerous practices could result from the lack of resources.

Some words are better avoided. In technical writing, the most common is probably 'done', as in 'the experiment was done', closely followed by 'split' when 'divided' is more appropriate (obviously, if you split the atom, that is the word you will use). A real-life example of both was found in an engineering report:

> The split of the system was done in two parts.

which probably means no more than:

> The system was divided in two.

or, possibly,

> The division of the system was carried out in two stages.

If technical writing is formal, as in a report, there is no place for personal comments. Occasionally, the writer feels so strongly about something that it seems impossible to leave it out, however inappropriate it is for the reader. 'I found these two interfaces both interesting and challenging to create,' a student engineer wrote, or, in an example found in company documentation, 'The process was held up because the company sent me on a course'. There may be a case for talking to the manager about these points, but they certainly should not be included in a report. The writing should be impersonal, without 'I' or 'you', and without any comment that shows the emotional state of the writer rather than the technical information required.

▶ 'Link' words and phrases

Readers need encouragement, especially that which comes from seeing how a passage is constructed. 'Link' words and phrases, which show a logical connection between sentences or paragraphs, guide the reader through the document, and incidentally help the flow of the writing. 'At the same time', 'on the other hand', 'meanwhile', 'bearing this in mind', and, correctly used, 'however', introduce the next stage of the argument. Some links add emphasis as well as flow; the earlier sentence about the engineers and the clients would read better with the addition of the small word 'even':

> Even the engineers involved in the project were unsure of the client's identity.

▶ 'Link' words and phrases guide the reader through the document and improve the flow of the writing

Activity 5.3 Linking words and phrases

This activity uses, with permission, a real-life example. A further passage from the engineering student's work on progressive failure has been rewritten with the logical connecting links omitted. It is awkward to read, and the information is not easy to assimilate. Try to add words and phrases that will improve this material. At the end of the book, the original version is given, and a comparison will show how much easier and more pleasant the latter is to read.

Structures which are highly optimised and operate at a high proportion of their ultimate load are most at risk from progressive failure. Obvious examples of this kind of structure are aerospace structures. Much attention has been paid in the design of airframes to ensuring fail-safety. Airframes have to have as low a weight as possible and are optimised to ensure that no part is larger than necessary. A variation from the assumed load pattern could have a serious effect on members close to the site of damage. Local damage would have this effect. Allowance must be made for this eventuality. Fail-safe or damage-tolerant design will remain serviceable after having been damaged. Alternative load paths are incorporated into the structure by means of multiple redundancy. When damage occurs, there are a number of other members which can carry the extra load.

▶ Writing persuasively

Linking words and phrases serve a further purpose. Not only do they make a passage more readable, but they also give emphasis, drawing the reader's attention to the most important aspects of the information. Combined with the guideline discussed earlier, putting the main point first in a sentence, they enable a writer to make a strong case while at the same time considering all the evidence. Activity 5.3 allows readers to see for themselves how this can come about.

Activity 5.4 Persuasive writing

Six pieces of information about shift work follow. Using this information, write a paragraph, assuming, first, that you are greatly in favour of shift work and want to convince your colleagues how worthwhile it is, without, of course, ignoring the arguments on the other side. Then write an alternative version: you are now just as strongly against shift work. Using exactly the same evidence, write to convince other people how damaging it is. In writing the two passages, use especially the two techniques mentioned above: order of words, and linking words and phrases.

1. Shift work gives you the opportunity to work in a small, dedicated group.
2. It has been suggested that shift work can lead to long-term health problems.
3. Shift work often allows you more variety and individual responsibility in your work.
4. Shift work makes normal family and social life difficult to achieve.
5. You may have extra holiday time and extra money by working shifts.
6. Shift work may isolate you from decision makers at work, and make it difficult to get help if you need it.

This chapter has included much good advice about style, but other important aspects are to be found in earlier chapters. At this point, therefore, the main points to remember have been brought together as a checklist to help you to achieve an appropriate, readable style.

► Checklist for good style in technical writing

- Use simple words as far as the complexity of the material allows
- Avoid irritating jargon; make every word add to the meaning or the ease of reading
- Keep the language formal: don't use *don't*, or *I* or *you*
- Write concisely and avoid waffle; never discuss your own feelings
- Vary the length of sentences, making sure that none is longer than about 40 words

- Use short sentences to highlight important information
- Balance the need for a unified structure to your paragraphs with encouragement for the reader
- Use lists whenever possible, numbering the items if the order is important
- Be precise, using words and figures to show accuracy of information
- Use a level of technical language that is appropriate to your readers
- Include linking words and phrases such as *therefore* and *at the same time*
- Decide the right way to convey each piece of information, whether by words, diagrams or mathematical material
- Use this checklist whenever you write!

▶ Summary

- ▶ Good style is appropriate to the needs of the reader
- ▶ Good style has its ABC: accuracy, brevity, clarity
- ▶ Use the active rather than the passive, whenever possible
- ▶ Follow national, international or professional conventions in presenting signs, symbols, units of measurement and abbreviations
- ▶ All tables, charts and diagrams must have numbers and titles for easy reference
- ▶ When using an equation editor, check accuracy from a printout
- ▶ Make the purpose of each equation clear and explain what each variable represents
- ▶ A well-chosen example helps the reader's understanding and gives life to the text
- ▶ References should show full and accurate bibliographical details, and should be consistent in form
- ▶ Avoid abstract words as far as possible. Use simple, direct language
- ▶ Listen critically to your own work
- ▶ 'Link' words and phrases guide the reader through the document and improve the flow of the writing
- ▶ Use this checklist whenever you write!

6 Writing for publication

Points covered ▶ **Writing articles**
▶ **Conference papers**
▶ **Writing reviews**
▶ **Writing books**
▶ **Avoiding prejudice**
▶ **Literary agents**

Nowadays, there is a tremendous outpouring of technical information, some of it online but a great deal still in the form of books, journals, the proceedings of conferences and specialist articles in the quality press. Such material all has to be written, and although much will be produced by professional journalists, there is a demand for the work of technical specialists, writing either as an optional extra or, especially in the case of academics, because it is part of their contract to write for publication.

This chapter is intended primarily for people who have not had material published before. It is a daunting prospect: most technical publications look authoritative and are often expensive; new writers understandably may feel that there is a great gulf between themselves and published authors.

Yet such would-be writers are themselves part of the market for technical publications, and they have no doubt assessed a range of work they use in order to keep up to date with their own field of interest. They probably know which journals are the most adventurous in publishing new ideas, which tend to lag behind the latest thinking; they may know a publisher whose technical books tend to carry authority, and they may have seen and been attracted by extracts or publicity on the internet. This is a useful start, as writing without a focus is rarely successful and the hopeful author needs to identify the publication which seems to suit the material available most closely.

▶ Writing articles

How to begin

The first stage for the hopeful writer is to analyse carefully what he or she wants to say. Is it the result of original research? Is it a response to something which was published earlier, perhaps a controversial article which merits wider discussion? Will the information be of specialist or general interest within the profession, or for intelligent lay readers?

In the light of the answers to these questions, the writer will need to consider the appropriate place for the proposed material. Should it appear in a **major refereed journal?** The advantages of this would be:

- It would be read by specialists in the same field, perhaps internationally
- Publication in such a journal would convey prestige and perhaps career enhancement to the writer
- The ideas put forward are likely to be discussed at a high level and any response will itself influence – for better or worse – the reputation of the writer.

There are, of course, also disadvantages:

- The editor is likely to receive a great deal of unsolicited material from hopeful beginners
- There may be established and well-known writers whose work will always have preference
- The refereeing system may mean that publication is delayed for a long time
- Referees may disapprove of the ideas in the article and may want major changes before agreeing to publication.

The writer may decide that it would be easier to start with a **more popular journal** in the field. Again, it is important to look at both sides of the question. The advantages are:

- The journal is likely to be published weekly or monthly, and so publication could be soon after submission
- The editor will need a good deal of material for such a frequent publication, and may therefore look kindly on a new writer

The article may reach a wider public (though possibly a less knowledgeable one) than a refereed journal; it may be more widely read in industry than an academic journal.

There are also disadvantages:

- The editor is likely to be interested in practical outcomes rather than pure research
- Sadly, some people can look down on what is perceived to be 'popular' journalism
- In academic circles, there may be little credit for an author who writes in a popular rather than a prestigious journal.

The would-be writer must consider which is the better type of publication to choose, in the light of the subject and the intended readership.

▶ Consider the subject, the probable readership and the type of journal you are aiming for

It is generally true that the more publications a writer has achieved, the easier it will be to get an article accepted. The first may well be the hardest. In view of this, there is something to be said for starting in the **letters pages** which most journals carry: a comment on a previous article, a personal experience which could have wider implications, a question that might lead to discussion – these are all ways of getting into print without the stress of a major article. Such a contribution should be of the length usually published (or shorter) and to the point – it is no good trying to occupy more space by rambling. If the letter is published and more correspondence follows, the writer will be noticed and the editor may be more willing to consider an article from someone whose name is familiar.

Choosing the journal

Once the writer has decided what sort of publication seems appropriate, the next step is to spend some time in the journals section of the company or university library. There are usually several examples of journals covering the right subject, and it is important to choose the right one to approach. Any one issue might not be typical, and so it is worth looking at two or three of each, and assessing:

- how prestigious the journal is, and whether articles are
- whether the coverage is specific to the writer's interest, or i.
- the length and depth of each article
- whether there has been a recent article on the same subject.

This last point may be good or bad: if interest has been generated
a discussion is developing, the editor might be pleased to have and
contribution, but if the subject has been aired widely in a recent issue, t.
editor might not want to approach it again for some time.

Colleagues may be able to give useful advice about likely journals,
especially if they themselves have had experience of writing for publication.

Once a possible journal has been selected, the writer needs to find the
answers to further questions:

- How long are the articles? (Count the number of words approximately.) Is there a range, for example a few long articles and a series
  of shorter 'taster' pieces?
- Who is the target readership and what is the style of the writing?
  Advice may be given on the editorial page, and the style of the articles
  may make it clear whether they are designed for a small number of
  highly specialised readers or for a range of interested people.
- What is the layout? Is the text arranged in columns or printed across the
  page? Text in columns needs to be written with shorter sentences and
  paragraphs than text across the page. Some journals provide templates for
  the layout of articles, and this has obvious advantages for a new writer.
- What type of diagrams are included? How are they labelled and numbered?
- Is there a list of references at the end of articles, and what is their format?

This information will help the writer to prepare an article that 'fits' the
journal, and therefore shows awareness of what is needed. The fewer
changes that the editor has to make, the more likely it is that the article
will be accepted.

This seems obvious, and yet too many writers start by writing an article
in the way they think best, without reference to what might be needed,
and they are then surprised (and offended) by rejection. Editors are busy
people, and, especially in journals that are not refereed, they have to
make rapid decisions. If an article looks as if it will need to be adapted, if
it is likely to go backwards and forwards between publisher and writer

several times, it is easier to reject it. The writer may see it as a precious piece of work, the result of hard labour, but to the editor it may be one of dozens. Always find out as much as possible about the journal, and then check that the specific article is suitable in its material and correct in its layout, using the template for this if there is one.

▶ Check the material and its layout in the chosen journal, and prepare the article in the same way

Making contact
It is essential to contact an appropriate person (probably but not necessarily the editor – see the first page of the journal itself) to find out in advance whether the article is likely to be considered, and ask for details of the house style. Sending an email with a short outline of the subject, its relevance to readers and the proposed length will probably result in a helpful response – the article may be of interest, in the form suggested or with a slightly different approach, or another journal might be more appropriate. Even if the editor is favourably inclined, a final decision may be made only after the full text is available, especially if the writer is unknown.

Most journals have detailed information which is available online or in hard copy to intending authors. This is likely to include a description of the specialist interest, the frequency of publication and the time this is likely to take, the procedure for refereeing if there is one, and the requirements of length and layout that the writer must adhere to. It will also give more specialised help with mathematical material and the computer packages that are suitable for the presentation of the artwork. If you are a member of a professional institution, you may be able to access extra advice for its publications, such as the *Guide for Authors* published by the Institution of Electrical Engineers.

▶ It is wise to contact editorial staff to discuss possible publication and obtain additional guidance

The writing process
The article can now be written in an appropriate style, with all this advice kept in mind. If the journal is aimed at industry rather than academics, the main point should be clear in the first paragraph, supported by good quality illustrations. A busy manager will probably glance at the page and pause to read only if his or her attention is caught. Academic readers are

more likely to feel obliged to read the whole of an article in their field of research.

Always write just short of the agreed length. If there is extra space to fill, it is easy to use out-takes or box a particular section; if the article is too long, it may be cropped by someone who is not an expert and the emphasis might be lost, or it might simply be rejected at once. Make the main message clear, with references if they are appropriate, and show the final version to one or two colleagues for their comments before submitting it.

▶ Always keep within the number of words stipulated by the editor

A long wait will probably follow submission, as the editor assesses not only the quality of the article but also how it might fit into a following issue. If it is to go out to referees, the wait will be particularly long; the writer might want to chase up progress by emailing the journal, but it would be unwise to do this too quickly or repeatedly. Eventually, there will be a message: the article might be accepted for publication as it stands, or it might need revision before it can be accepted, or it might be rejected, with or without comment.

If it is accepted, the author may or may not get page proofs; these will need to be checked quickly, by the date stipulated. Only minor changes can be made at this stage, and the writer would be well advised to avoid amendments that affect the layout of the page (unless, of course, the original error was the printer's; this is less likely now that the author will probably have submitted the article in electronic form as well as a hard copy). If the referees or the editor make suggestions, these must be taken seriously (referees will be known experts in the subject), although in the last resort a writer can withdraw the article if the changes are felt to be totally unacceptable and no compromise is possible

Rejections are hard on the writer. If the editor has made helpful comments, this is encouraging, as it would not be likely to happen if the article were entirely without merit. The implied message is that the article has some potential, but it might not be right for this particular journal at this time. Any advice given must be seen in a positive light: it may make acceptance easier in the future. Most authors experience rejection at some stage, usually early in their careers; it is unpleasant but a useful learning experience!

▶ Conference papers

The first form of publication available to young engineers, especially in academic life, is often in the papers of a conference at which they have spoken. Most conference organisers want a printed version that can become a lasting record of what was said, and this is obviously in the interests of the speaker.

There is a major problem with this form of dissemination: notes which were ideal during the actual presentation are rarely suitable for publication as they stand. This inherent difficulty is made worse nowadays by the habit of asking speakers to send in a copy of the PowerPoint slides used, regardless of the fact that a message on the screen, which is clear as the speaker talks through it, may be meaningless without that spoken input. The engineer who finds himself or herself in this position should offer a 'written' text and fuller versions of the slides which will convey the sense more completely and clearly than the originals. It is worth asking if this problem is going to arise before the conference takes place, so that the speaker, in preparing the talk, can at the same time write a fuller version for publication. The word 'fuller' is used deliberately: there may be complex material, particularly mathematical or highly technical detail, which cannot sensibly be included in a presentation but which could be made available to the audience through the printed text. It is also worth remembering that a speaker might want to modify or adapt what was said in the light of the discussion that followed, and there should be an opportunity for this. (For a more detailed analysis of the needs of a presenter as opposed to a writer, see the author's book *Effective Communication for Science and Technology* in Further reading on page 143.)

▶ A conference paper is generally best produced in two versions, one to be spoken and a fuller one for publication

▶ Writing reviews

The opportunity to prepare a review or a longer review article is sometimes open to an engineer with highly specialised knowledge. It is true that editors like to have a recognised name at the end of such an article, but it is not always possible to find one, especially if time is short. It is worth letting an appropriate editor know that there is a writer who has expert knowledge within the field covered by the journal and who would be willing to write a review occasionally. Obviously, all the advice given above about following the editor's guidelines also applies here.

Publishers also need expert reviewers to comment on material submitted for publication. It is unlikely that such an opportunity would occur often, but it may be worth letting a publisher who specialises in the same area of work know that there is someone with the right expertise who can be called on. In writing such a review, it is important to be as impartial as possible and write in a balanced way, with criticism backed up by examples, however strongly the reviewer feels about the author's handling of the subject.

▶ Writing books

A great deal of technical information is published in articles, conference papers and on the internet, the last of these being a particularly rapid means of disseminating new ideas. Books present a greater difficulty, as they take much longer to write, and the time between the end of the writing and the book's publication is also considerable, probably a year or even more; books also go out of date comparatively quickly. Writing a book is therefore not a good method of either letting the world know about a new and brilliant piece of engineering research or trying to reach future generations of students.

Nevertheless, we have all been educated and trained partly through the use of books, and today's academic researcher especially is unlikely to get far in his or her career without publishing at least one well-received book.

How to begin

The first stages of preparing a book are similar to those for an article, except that the writer is now looking at a range of publishers and deciding which covers the right area of work and is highly esteemed by other experts. Publishers tend to specialise, not only in their subject coverage but also in the level at which their books are aimed: some will focus on an advanced research market, while others will be aiming for schools or undergraduates. Major publishers may cover both levels, but they will have different editors in charge of each.

Publishers are usually interested in discovering new authors, and it is worthwhile contacting the appropriate commissioning editor and arranging a meeting. However, it is essential to be well prepared. No editor would want to be presented with a complete manuscript ready for publication (unless the writer is a well-established major author in the field, and maybe not even then). Most authors need the advice and support of their editors, and this initial meeting can be crucial in building a good relationship.

Writing a proposal

The publisher will need a written proposal. In preparing it, the writer must analyse what is to be achieved and what the target readership is – a necessary and useful stage, as it helps the author to focus on exactly what will be written, at what level and in what form. If possible, the proposal should be emailed to the commissioning editor before the first meeting, so that it can be discussed in detail.

The proposal should include as much as possible of the following information.

Market
The intended readership, in categories if appropriate (students, specialists, general readers, etc)
An assessment of the size of that readership, with an idea of its range (national, Western European, international) if possible

Content
A synopsis of the book, with chapter headings and an indication of the content of each chapter
A rationale describing why the book is needed, with any new features or approaches
A sample chapter, unless the writer's earlier work has already been published
An estimate of the length of the book

Competition
A brief analysis of competing books on the market, with an assessment of the advantages of the current proposal

The author
A brief note about the author, stressing expertise and any previous publications

---

This proposal will be sent to experts in the area of knowledge and they will assess the need for the book and its value to the readership and the publisher. The reviews they prepare will be sent anonymously to the author, and the comments are usually helpful in showing where improvements can be made in order to make the book more marketable. The author does not have to accept the suggestions, but it is worth having a very good reason for rejecting them.

The commissioning editor will probably have given the writer a copy of the guide for authors, giving similar information to that provided to writers of articles, but with particular stress on the laws of copyright. The author is responsible for providing proof that permission has been obtained to use other published sources (for instance for quotations), and it is wise to discuss the current requirements of the law with the editor at an early stage.

A contract will be drawn up between the author and the publisher, with details about rights and responsibilities on both sides. This is of course a legally binding document, and advice may be needed before the author signs. It is also sensible to think carefully about the date given for receipt of the typescript (and disk); publishers rarely mind if the book arrives early, but they are not at all happy if it is late.

Writing a book is a long process, and the editor will try to keep in touch from time to time to see how the work is progressing and give help or advice. It is wise as well as courteous to let the publisher know as soon as possible if there is a major problem which will delay the typescript beyond the agreed date; books are often advertised long before they are actually produced, and an unexpected delay can cause a series of difficulties within the company.

▶ Prepare a book proposal and, if possible, meet the commissioning editor before starting to write. Keep in touch for queries and advice

In time, the author will receive a copy-edited version of the book, followed by proofs (sometimes a second set of proofs is provided). No major changes should be made at these stages, but the author does have the chance to look for any details that have slipped through and need correction. There will at some point also be a copy of the cover design and proofs of the cover, and of course the latter should be checked carefully. Conventional proofreading symbols should be followed, but if a correction is complicated, it is worth writing out the section and adding it with a note to the copy editor so that it is clear.

Book production is a long process, but the thrill that accompanies the arrival of an advance copy makes it all worthwhile.

▶ Avoiding prejudice

There are some constraints on what an author writes which must be followed because legal action would follow if they were ignored: seditious, racist or 'offensive' (however that is interpreted) material would rightly be rejected by the publisher. Nowadays, it is important to avoid sexism: a writer can usually employ the plural or turn a sentence round instead of using 'he or she', although, as a careful reader of this book will have noticed, this rather cumbersome expression can be used from time to time.

There is, however, another area of prejudice that an author might not be aware of. It is easy to write exclusively for one's own culture. If the book is for national consumption only, this will not matter, but if the intended readership is international, the wording might need to be changed (other countries have finance ministers rather than chancellors of the exchequer), and some examples or case studies might be based on non-UK material, as long as the meaning is clear to all users. Many engineers throughout the world have some of their engineering education and training in English, but an international writer will try to avoid colloquialisms which would only puzzle overseas readers – 'letting the cat out of the bag' would seem very odd to anyone who hadn't met the expression before!

▶ Literary agents

Contrary to popular opinion, it is not only bestselling novelists who use the services of literary agents! They can help the author to find the right publisher and make the initial approach, they draw up contracts which cover eventualities that most writers would never think of, they can be a tower of strength if there is a dispute between writer and publisher, and they are on the author's side, providing advice, support and encouragement.

Having said this, it is only right to add that literary agents are unlikely to be enthusiastic about a totally unknown author, or a writer who only ever writes one book. Academic writers often seek advice from one another, and may earn very little in the way of royalties. Nevertheless, there are technical writers who want to write regularly and who might produce a bestselling textbook or a widely read volume on a topical issue, and such writers, even if they have had little experience to date, might benefit from using an agent. The latest issue of the *Writers' and Artists' Yearbook* gives advice about agents and their areas of specialism, along with help in approaching them. Agents take a percentage of the author's royalties, but their support and advice can be worth a great deal more.

Writing for publication can be hard work but very rewarding, not least in the pleasure gained from helping to disseminate technical information to a wide and enthusiastic readership.

▶ Summary

- ▶ Consider the subject, the probable readership and the type of journal you are aiming for
- ▶ Check the material and its layout in the chosen journal, and prepare the article in the same way
- ▶ It is wise to contact editorial staff to discuss possible publication and obtain additional guidance
- ▶ Always keep within the number of words stipulated by the editor
- ▶ A conference paper is generally best produced in two versions, one to be spoken and a fuller one for publication
- ▶ Prepare a book proposal and, if possible, meet the commissioning editor before starting to write. Keep in touch for queries and advice

7 The presentation of written information

▶ The importance of good presentation

Earlier in this book (Chapter 4), we looked at the formats appropriate to emails, letters, reports and instructions, and at the conventions of style and layout which should be followed. There is another aspect, however, of the effectiveness of written information: its presentation. This is largely a matter of reader goodwill. If the document looks both professional and inviting, the reader will want to read it. If it looks scruffy and difficult to approach, the prospective reader will be put off, and will relegate the paper to the bottom of the pile, or, worse, the wastepaper basket. A report which looks less than professional undermines the credibility of both writer and company; instructions which do not look 'official' may be ignored.

In this chapter, two different aspects of presentation are discussed: checking (to make sure that the correct information is correctly presented) and the layout of the printed page.

▶ Checking the facts

Most documents are checked for factual errors. Before starting to write, an author may need to make reference to previous similar documents, company guidelines, and books and journals in a library belonging to the company or a professional institution. Later, the writer will go back over the document, to make sure that its contents are technically correct and in accordance with company policy. A colleague's opinion may well be sought. In the case of a report or specification, a draft version is likely to be passed up the hierarchy of the author's organisation so that it can be checked by more senior managers. In passing, it is worth mentioning that any changes made should always be for a good reason. Too many documents are subjected to a manager's need to 'make his/her mark' (the subconscious 'if I don't alter something, how can I show that I'm doing my job/how can I show how important my opinion is?' response). Nevertheless, it is generally true that this stage is valuable in order to ensure that the document contains the right information logically presented, and that it is within the limits of what may be revealed; this is especially true when company confidentiality or security is involved.

In the case of instructions, the most sensible way to check what has been written is to ask a colleague to carry out the procedure under the writer's supervision; if a stage has been omitted or the wording is not clear, the problem should be immediately apparent. It is, of course, wise to choose a colleague who does not normally carry out such instructions, or the correct action might be taken automatically despite instructions to the contrary.

▶ All documents should be checked for factual accuracy

▶ Checking the text

The second stage of checking is often overlooked. The facts are assembled and the correct information has been obtained, but what appears on the page is not what the writer intended. Most engineers nowadays write directly onto the computer. They remain physically and mentally close to what they are producing; it is there in front of them, available for revision, additions or deletions at any time. The writer knows perfectly well what was intended, to the point where he or she will see it even if it isn't there.

We are all bad at checking our own work. Our interest and involvement is with the information, not with the actual writing, and it is all far too familiar to us. We fail to see what has gone wrong. There are two results of this failure, and both are serious for the individual and the company in whose name the document is to be sent out. The first is that incorrect data are passed on to the reader (colleague, client, general public). It is easy to imagine the impact of a nought missed off the end of a price in an estimate or an invoice. It is impossible to guess at the amount of time and money wasted annually in telephone calls, meetings and discussions which take place to find out what is wrong with the product, system or payment, all because nobody bothered to check the original wording and notice the mistake. It must run into millions of pounds. In the case of engineering information, the results of error may be even worse, in terms of industrial accidents and personal injury.

The second result of the failure to check what has been written is almost as serious, but even harder to quantify. It is the loss of professional credibility. The reader is, after all, taking for granted the expertise of the engineer who produced the document. Readers will order equipment on the basis of the information given; they will become involved with costly projects or stake the reputation of their companies or even their lives on the accuracy of the details they have been given. As soon as they see a mistake, however small and insignificant it may be in itself, they will start to worry about the accuracy of everything else. This is particularly true of mathematical information. If a letter in a word is misplaced or omitted, readers may well be able to guess what the word should be. The lasting effect of, for example, two letters transposed in a word, is to make readers doubt *every figure* in the writer's specification, quotation or test report. Everything is suspect and therefore potentially unreliable.

▶ Keyboarding errors distort information and undermine credibility

▶ All documents should be checked for accuracy of presentation

There is no easy or complete answer to the problem of keyboarding errors. Computers have built-in spellchecks, which are helpful provided they are not used as the only form of checking. They will highlight nonsense words, but not the wrong word which makes sense or which is common throughout the document. 'Now' instead of 'not' is an outstanding example of the dangerous mistake which the spellcheck will ignore. It reverses the meaning and yet appears to make complete sense, as in:

The car is now safe to drive.
The car is not safe to drive.

This critical error will be picked up only by an alert human reader.

Ideally, every document should be checked specifically for such errors. In practice, the level of checking will depend on the perceived importance of the document concerned. Short emails and other comparatively casual writing may be checked quickly on the screen and as a printout, and this is probably sufficient. All reports and similar documents which travel outside the company, and all specifications, instructions and manuals, should be thoroughly checked for errors of writing as a separate activity from checking the facts. It is dangerous simply to combine these two operations, as inevitably the facts will appear to be more important. The best person to check the text itself is almost certainly a colleague who is familiar with the sort of information presented, without being an expert on the immediate subject discussed; it is important that this reader will not make assumptions about the writer's meaning. Diagrams, appendices and equations (the last of these particularly difficult to check) must be included in the checking process. The title page is often overlooked, partly because it is assumed to be correct and partly because it usually contains capital letters, which are difficult to read and which the spellcheck may not handle efficiently. Needless to say, an error on the title page, the first part of the document that readers are likely to look at, is particularly serious in its implications.

Activity 7.1 Checking

The following passage contains a number of deliberate mistakes. Some will be identified by the computer and others will not. Try to identify them all, and then compare your list with the suggested version at the end of the book.

Most industrial sheds in the aria are strategically placed on the industrial estate well away from from the town and towards the motorway. From the mid-1980s, developement also took place on the old railway sidings. The single-story units are usually large and open-plan. Styles vary form brick units with large shutters and few windows to large corrigated or plane metal units with a skeletal frame and now widows. Maintenance is slow, as is rent. Refurbishment is easy, and may units incorporate a mezzanine level. The local area is wide and flat and allows for easy packing and good delivery facilities.

▶ The need for consistency

Inconsistency has a similar effect in that it suggests a casual, slipshod approach to the writing. It is usually unimportant whether a writer chooses 's' or 'z' in a word like 'organisation', but a change of mind in the middle of the document undermines the reader's confidence. Even apparently trivial decisions, such as to use the more common 'eg' rather than 'e.g.' must be made consistently, and must be consistent also with one another, so that if 'eg' is used, 'etc' will not have a full stop either. Part of the process of checking is to watch for inconsistency, and, sensibly, to record decisions about usage as they are taken. This is particularly important if the document is produced by a group of people, some of whom might, for example, use 'subcontractors' rather than the slightly old-fashioned form 'sub-contractors'. One member of the group should have editorial responsibility for making such decisions and notifying other writers early in the production of the document; checking will then be made easier.

▶ Consistency suggests conscientiousness and reassures the reader

The first stage of checking will always be the duty of the writer. If the text can be left alone for a couple of days, or preferably a week, the author is much more likely to see mistakes than if checking started only five minutes after the printout was produced. Checking is a time-consuming job (lack of time is the most common 'excuse' for not checking), and it is a mistake either to leave insufficient time to be thorough or assume that a 'spare hour' can be devoted at the end to going through the complete document. The timespan for concentration is short, especially as checking is boring as well as time-consuming, and the writer should take regular short breaks. Even a couple of minutes spent every quarter of an hour in leaning back and looking out of the window will help.

A document should always be checked not only on the screen but also from a printout – a page flat on the desk is at a much more normal reading angle than a screen. A helpful technique is to put a blank piece of paper over the text and reveal one line at a time. It is unlikely that a single line will make complete sense, and so the writer is able to concentrate on the words rather than the meaning. Some mistakes are particularly difficult to see, such as the duplication or omission of an 'unimportant' word like 'the', or the creation of a word which has the same shape as the word intended, such as 'casual' for 'causal' or 'form' for 'from'.

Computers are a wonderful invention, but they can produce their own problems. Just because it is so easy to correct a mistake, the writer whose inspiration is in full flow will tend to leave the correction until later, when the mistake may be forgotten or much less obvious. As material is moved around, it may no longer be consistent with what now comes before it, so that a singular subject may end up with a plural verb and so on. The insertion of an extra paragraph will move other material on to different pages, and a heading may be separated from the text to which it refers, or a key word at the end of a sentence may now be on a separate page from its context. The task of checking includes making sure that such irritations have been removed.

▶ Page layout

Layout on the page can make both reading and checking easier or more difficult. A right-justified text, in which all lines end at the same point, creating a regular right-hand margin, may look attractive – although opinions vary – but it is harder to read and check than unjustified ('ragged right') text. If numbers are included in a long paragraph, it is particularly important that the eye can move accurately from the end of one line to the beginning of the next, and is not allowed to jump a line.

▶ Right-hand justification should be avoided if possible

▶ Choice of font

The font chosen should be simple and undecorated (Times New Roman is popular if a font with serifs is chosen; Arial is a useful sans-serif font). It should also be large enough for ease of reading. On the whole, 12 point is a sensible size, with normal single interline spacing; if mathematical material is included, special care should be taken to ensure that superscript and subscript figures do not corrupt the lines of text. In printing an early draft of the document, the writer may choose double spacing in order to have room to make notes at the appropriate point on the printout, but it will be a little harder to read in the finished product.

▶ Line length

Line length should also be checked. Ideally, the number of key strokes to a line of print should be between 80 and 100; if there are more than this, the reader's eyes cannot move easily from the end of one line to the beginning of the next, and the text will be perceived as heavy to read, although the reader may well not know why this is so.

▶ Font style and size, and line length, should be chosen for the reader's convenience

▶ The use of space

The need for space has been stressed several times in this book. The layout of the page should look well spaced, with appropriate gaps between words, lines, paragraphs or sections, and round the edges of the text. Margin space on the left is important so that words or figures are not lost in the binding, and there should be adequate space at the top and bottom of the page; a minimum of half an inch (just over 1 cm) is suggested for printed material and twice that amount for wordprocessed text. A congested page looks unattractive and heavy, and is unlikely to encourage the reader.

▶ Leave space on the page to allow the text to stand out clearly

▶ Title pages

The title page is usually the first page of a document which the reader sees. Title pages give status as well as administrative information. Manuals, instructions, specifications and reports have title pages, which contain standard information: title, author and date. A reference number may also be required, together with the issuing company's logo, name and address. Similar details of the client company for whom the document was produced will be included as appropriate. A statement of confidentiality or copyright information should be shown if it is needed. All these details are often specified in the company's templates, but the individual engineer may be able to ensure that the layout of the title page is uncluttered and gives a professional look to the whole document.

▶ A well-laid out title page gives a professional appearance to the whole document

Many reports and similar documents will be photocopied, at least in part. At this stage, the value of numbering the pages is apparent – it is too easy for unnumbered pages to be omitted by accident. Poor quality copying can make figures unclear or ambiguous, and checking one set of copied material is a good idea.

▶ Binding

Binding is the last stage in the completion of most documents. The style of binding may be laid down by the company, but the choice should be made in the light of the document's importance, length and longevity. Stapling is inappropriate for all but the shortest in-company documentation: the last page is easily torn off, and the rule seems to apply that the staple itself will go through the most important word on the second page. A slide bar binding, usually chosen by students because it is cheap and can be reused, has the disadvantage that pages will not lie flat on the desk, and the slide bar itself is likely to come off, allowing the pages to fall apart. Spiral bindings are widely used: they will lie flat on the table in use, are secure and on the whole look attractive. They are not sensible for very short or very long reports, and if several documents are kept on a shelf together, the spirals can become entangled. Ring binders are more bulky but useful for material which will have to be updated regularly; they have the associated disadvantage that it is all too easy for people to remove pages or sections without permission.

Other more permanent forms of binding tend to be reserved for major documents which have a long lifespan in printed form, or which are intended primarily to impress a client. Indeed, some documents would benefit from being professionally designed. If the information is to be used commercially, is expensive to obtain or the company's professional image is at stake, it is worth making sure that the cover design is both attractive and effective, so that the document makes the strongest possible impact on the recipient. Major published reports are clearly in this category.

▶ Both overall design and binding should be appropriate to the impact which the document is intended to make

▶ Attractive and professional text

However the final document is produced, it should look and feel good in use. In the light of advances in technology, it may seem surprising that this is still so true; we might have been living by now with the 'paperless office' we once expected, so that all documents are held only on computers. In practice, this has not yet happened. Documents are produced and updated by computer and generally transmitted electronically, but they are still usually printed out to be read, and passed on to other readers in book form. The impact of a document remains important. It should attract the attention of its readers and users by its attractive appearance, clear helpful format, accuracy of presentation, and precise, unambiguous written style. The effect should always be one of pleasure and reassurance, that time and trouble have been taken to produce a document worthy of its technical content.

▶ A document should look both attractive and professional; it should inspire confidence in its readers

▶ Summary

▶ All documents should be checked for factual accuracy
▶ Keyboarding errors distort information and undermine credibility
▶ All documents should be checked for accuracy of presentation
▶ Consistency suggests conscientiousness and reassures the reader
▶ Right-hand justification should be avoided if possible
▶ Font style and size, and line length, should be chosen for the reader's convenience
▶ Leave space on the page to allow the text to stand out clearly
▶ A well-laid out title page gives a professional appearance to the whole document
▶ Both overall design and binding should be appropriate to the impact which the document is intended to make
▶ A document should look both attractive and professional; it should inspire confidence

Comments on and solutions to activities

▶ Chapter 2

2.1 Prefixes
- *Ambi* means *both*, as in *ambidextrous, ambiguity*
- *Homo* means *the same*, as in *homologous, homonym*
- *Mal* means *bad*, as in *malevolent, malformation*
- *Meta* means *change*, as in *metamorphic, metaplasm*
- *Retro* means *backwards*, as in *retroact, retro-rocket*

2.2 Word confusion
The station**a**ry vehicle was the princip**al** cause of the traffic jam. Motorists were advi**s**ed to find a different route until the police could **e**ffect a solution to the problem. Later, some **implied** that the authorities had been **un**interested until the chief constable's car had been delayed, a charge that was strenuously **denied** but **cited** the next day in the papers.

2.3 Inaccurate writing
Members of the team **attempted** to **start** the process, but could not **see how to proceed**. Their position was **made worse** by the **number** of software problems for which they **could not devise** solutions. They were told to try again with **fewer** people involved, and were **finally successful**, avoiding the **expected crisis**.

▶ Chapter 3

3.1 Overlong sentence
Engineers who work very long hours may suffer health problems in the long term. This is especially true if their work is particularly

intensive, involving responsibility for younger and less experienced staff, and the use of delicate machinery. Employers need to be aware of the increased risk of accidents.

Notice that the main point is now in a shorter sentence (14 words), and the new aspect, the employer's responsibility, is also in a separate sentence (11 words). The repetition of 'intensive' and 'intense' has been avoided, and unnecessary expressions such as 'who need a great deal of supervision' have been omitted ('responsibility' covers the point adequately). 'Unwise' is a weak expression in this context.

3.2 Organising a sentence
Version 1, emphasising the weight of the rigs: *The weight of the rigs necessitated the use of a tow truck.*
Version 2, emphasising the need for a tow truck: *A tow truck was needed because of the weight of the rigs.*

3.3 Redundant words
The original sentence is repeated below, with unnecessarily wordy material highlighted. Sometimes this is a single word, such as 'originally', as the design stage must have been at the beginning; at times, a whole phrase can go, such as 'to the detriment of residents' – congestion and pollution are inevitably to their detriment. There is then a suggested version of the passage.

The road was **originally** designed with **the needs of** residential users predominantly in mind, although **over a number of years an element of** commercial use, **much of which consists of** retail properties, has **come into existence.** If **an additional amount of** traffic is generated, as **it well might be if** the current proposal **is implemented, problems of** increased congestion and **even more** pollution would **inevitably** result, **to the detriment of residents**.

The road was designed mainly for residential users, although there has been some commercial development, mainly retail. The current proposal would be likely to increase both traffic congestion and pollution.

3.4 Overcomplicated writing

1. *(Please) note that reports should show both the resource require-ments for any activity which has overrun, and the normal requirements for the current period.*
2. *The project group has decided to resume work with the original design, since it might not otherwise be possible to get beyond the prototype stage.*

3.5 Punctuation

Businesspeople are more likely to take the train, it seems, if the total journey time is three hours or less. However, if it's longer than that, they will consider flying. It's a pity that train journeys are so often plagued by mobile phones, an ever-increasing menace, especially to those who would like a peaceful journey on which to read, use their laptops or, in extreme cases, go to sleep. At least nowadays there is the occasional quiet coach where it's possible to escape from the mobile and its noisy users.

▶ Chapter 4

4.1 Email

This email is not always sufficiently informative ('I need to know' – when?, what if 'I' am not available?), and its structure is not clear or easy to follow. In order to keep a good format, it would be better to send a short message by email, telling the students in the group that they must read the attachment (and perhaps insisting that they sign to say that they have read it, in the next class). The essential information could then be properly formatted in the attachment.

At present, its appearance is heavy and there are stylistic failings in the writing, as follows:

1. 'remembering': who remembers? Presumably the student, rather than 'I'.
2. 'them' (line 4): this appears to refer to 'special precautions', but the sense would suggest that it refers to 'hazards', which is much earlier in the paragraph.

3. 'Watch out for' is inappropriate style: how can anyone 'watch out for' electric shock? There is no information about first aid assistance if anyone suffered an electric shock. 'and insulation and protection' is just added without being clearly associated with the rest of the sentence.
4. The list of hazards is written along the line rather than as a list; it includes 'where you intend to keep fire extinguishers', which is clearly not a hazard but a digression.
5. 'they must be protected against': against what? The sentence is the wrong way round.
6. The contrast of 'the first time' and 'every time' is badly placed, so that the significance of the latter is hidden.
7. No attempt has been made to give emphasis to particularly important information.

Attachment to email: suggested version

Student projects: essential safety issues

Please let me know before the end of October the hazards associated with your project and the steps you propose to take in order to safeguard against them.

In particular, you should be aware of the following hazards:

1. *Electric shock*: insulation and protection must be adequate.
2. *Fire*: notify me of the position of fire extinguishers and other fire-fighting equipment.
3. *Pressurised or other highly stressed components*: protection in the case of failure must be adequate.
4. *Moving components*, such as rotating shafts, gears, belts, pulleys: guards must be in place.
5. *Sharp projections, dropped objects etc.* may cause injury from falling or tripping. Take care at all times, for yourselves and for other people.

If apparatus is used away from supervised areas, special precautions must be taken; contact me in advance.

(Cont'd)

Your project supervisor must be present:

1. whenever hazardous apparatus is used for the first time
2. *always* if the apparatus is rated 'very hazardous'.

If you have safety problems or queries, contact me on extension 274 (room 34B); if I am not available, you must speak to the Departmental Safety Officer before starting work.

You will be given details of staff qualified in first aid and the action to be taken in an emergency before your projects begin.

Jim Twigg, First Year Tutor

4.2 Short report and covering letter

The information in this passage is written in one long paragraph, with no attempt to identify the tests carried out, the results or the comments. It is difficult to decide what is fact and what is suggestion. Headings, sections and the use of space will make a great difference to the reader's comprehension. For these reasons, the most helpful format is probably a brief report sent with a short covering letter.

The letter is set out according to the conventions given on pages 68–9, signed and dated. The heading draws the reader's attention immediately to the subject, and the essential test results are given at once. There is, of course, some overlap with the report itself, but this enables the reader to take in the key message before he has time to consider the report as a whole. If he chooses to pass on the report to a colleague, he still has this message in the letter itself.

It has been assumed that writer and reader are known to each other, and the tone is therefore friendly but formal. The letter gives the writer the opportunity to add the kind of detail which would be inappropriate in the report – in this case, that she or a colleague will phone to discuss the action to be taken as a result of the report. The addition of 'Best wishes' before the close of the letter reflects a good working relationship and, perhaps, the desire that it should continue.

The report is equally formal, and the use of the first person in the original passage has disappeared. In the case of such a short report, it might not be thought necessary to number the headings; with a longer report, they would certainly be numbered (see p. 73).

Covering letter: suggested version

---

29 May 2004

Mr S Jenkins
General Manager
Meredith Jenkins & Sons Limited
Station Road
Denfield
Yorkshire SH1 6DJ

Dear Mr Jenkins

76 mm diameter swaged tube, as supplied

On 27 May, Richard MacNamara and I carried out a push-out test on the swaged tube, as agreed. Details of the test, the results and our comments are given in the enclosed report.

As you will see, the results we obtained confirm that there is a problem with the jointing system as proposed. We feel that more consideration should be given to the strength of the weld before the series of pull-out tests commences; as you know, these will be expensive. However, our preliminary work suggests that savings could be made by the use of mild steel instead of 826M40 (EN26).

We would strongly recommend that further push-out tests be carried out as soon as practicable. Either Richard or I will ring you in a couple of days to discuss the best way for us to proceed.

Best wishes

Yours sincerely
Sarah Watson
Sarah Watson, Development Engineer

Short report: suggested version

Introduction

In accordance with instructions received from Mr Simon Jenkins of Meredith Jenkins & Sons Limited, Richard MacNamara and Sarah Watson, Development Engineers, carried out a preliminary push-out test on the 76 mm diameter swaged tube supplied. The test was requested because of uncertainty about the suitability of the tube for the proposed jointing system.

The test was conducted on 27 May 2004 at the Research and Development workshop at Denfield.

Test procedure

A plaster cast of the inside of the tube was made, and a steel plug machined to match the cast. The plug was forced through the tube, which was held by a plate welded round the edge, in a compression testing machine.

The effect on the swaged tube was similar to that intended for the planned pull-out test.

Results

The tube failed at a load of 218 kN by the cracking of the longitudinal weld, which had previously been ground flat on the inside, after very little distortion.

Comments

This result appears to confirm a difficulty with the proposed jointing system, and it is not clear how it could easily be overcome. The failure load of 218 kN gives a factor of safety of only 1.3 over the normal working load of 168 kN in axial tension.

Recommendations

1. Further push-out tests should be carried out on other samples in order to confirm the figure of 218 kN.
2. Consideration should be given to the weld strength problem before a more expensive series of pull-out tests is started. The components for the pull-out tests include 826M40 (EN26) steel,

---

since failure might require a swaging load of over 600kN, and the fittings have been designed for the thickest available tubes of 168mm outside diameter (10mm wall).

3. Mild steel appears to be suitable for such tests, and would reduce the cost. Its use is therefore recommended.

Richard MacNamara
Sarah Watson
29 May 2004

4.3 Long report

This is not a report, but an essay. It has no headings and lacks any clear structure. One set of measurements is given as a table, while the other is hidden within the text, and it is not easy to pick out background information as opposed to the current test. Sections of information cannot be quickly identified, and the reader would find it difficult to use the table at the end when reading the main text. Conclusions and recommendations are confused, and the report seems to peter out with no clear statement of what action should be taken. There is no summary to give the reader an overall view of the essential message of the report; as a basis for discussion and action, it leaves much to be desired.

The information can be organised into a conventional report format with a summary and a clear logical structure, as follows.

Report: suggested version

The effect of acoustic ceiling tiles on noise at the County Swimming Pools, Northwich, February 2003

Summary
In response to a request from the Council, Dr Andrew Poynter assessed the effectiveness of the acoustic tiles which had been fitted in 2002 to the ceiling of the Learner Pool at the County Swimming Pool, Northwich. Reverberation times and noise levels were found to have fallen significantly, giving additional

(Cont'd)

directional information and speech intelligibility. Safety had been increased and staff working conditions had improved.

It is recommended that the Council should consider using similar tiles to extend the area of the acoustic ceiling.

1. Background

During 2001, Northwich Borough Council identified a problem with noise levels in the Learner Pool at the County Swimming Pools, Northwich. Dr Andrew Poynter, Senior Lecturer in Engineering at the University of Abimouth, carried out a series of tests to ascertain both the reverberation times at different frequencies and the noise level, when an average weekend attendance of 35 people was present. The results of these tests were given in the report and are reproduced in Tables 1 and 2.

As a result of these tests, it was recommended that acoustic tiles manufactured by Fraser and Macfarlane should be fitted to $114\,m^2$ of the ceiling area, with the expectation that there would be an improvement in both reverberation times and noise levels. The predictions of both Andrew Poynter and the manufacturer's representative are also given in Tables 1 and 2.

The tiles were fitted in November 2002. In January 2003 the Council asked Andrew Poynter to assess the effect of the new ceiling.

2. Assessment of acoustic ceiling

On 1 February 2003, Andrew Poynter inspected the new acoustic ceiling. As on the previous occasion, there were approximately 35 people using the pool.

The investigation showed that the tiles had been fitted to an area measuring $180\,m^2$ instead of $114\,m^2$. The backing of the tiles, fibre glass in film bags, was not precisely the same as that tested earlier. The predictions were therefore not accurate, but gave a sufficient indication of the changes which might have been expected. Reverberation times and noise levels were again measured.

2.1 Reverberation measurement

The reverberation times were measured and compared with those of the untreated ceiling and with the predictions made by Dr Poynter and by a representative of the tile manufacturers. The results are given in Table 1.

Table 1   Reverberation times in the Learner Pool (curtain open)

Frequency (Hz)	2001 (seconds)	A. Poynter's recommendation (seconds)	Fraser & Mcfarlane's prediction* (seconds)	2003 (seconds)
125	1.75	–	2.8	0.7
250	2.2	–	2.0	0.4
500	2.4	1.5	1.3	0.55
1000	3.8	1.65	1.5	0.8
2000	3.6	1.65	1.7	0.85
4000	3.0	1.5	1.6	0.9
8000	–	–	–	0.55

* Fraser & Macfarlane's prediction was based upon $114\,m^2$ of treatment whereas the actual area installed was $180\,m^2$.

2.2 Noise level measurements

The noise levels were then measured, and compared with those recorded for the untreated ceiling. The results are given in Table 2.

Table 2   Noise levels

	Untreated ceiling (dBA)	Acoustic ceiling (dBA)
Average	92	77
Maximum	103	87
Minimum	87	71

2.3 Discussions with staff

The effect of the new ceiling tiles was discussed with attendants and instructors at the Learner Pool. They reported that the intelligibility of speech had greatly improved, increasing both the response to training and therefore safety. The overall sound level had been reduced, which was beneficial to staff, and they were better able to identify the direction of noise, which again was a safety factor. Overall, they were delighted with the new ceiling.

(Cont'd)

---

3. Conclusions

As a result of the investigations described, Andrew Poynter came to the following conclusions:

1. Reverberation times were shorter than expected, perhaps because of the structure of the backing of the tiles.
2. Noise levels had fallen considerably.
3. As a result of 2, safety has been improved both by an increase in directional information and by improvement in speech intelligibility. The work of attendants and instructors has been made easier and pleasanter.

4. Recommendations

In the light of these conclusions, it is recommended that the Council should consider extending the area of acoustic tiles, and that, if this were to be done, the same type of tiles should be used.

Andrew Poynter, BSc, PhD, C.Eng
Department of Mechanical Engineering
University of Abimouth
5 February 2003

4.4 Instructions

The instructions in this activity are written as continuous prose and are therefore difficult to use. The particular problems which an engineer would face in trying to follow the information are given below:

1. The instructions are given as one 56-word sentence.
2. 'First of all' is wordy; stages should be given numbers.
3. Users are told that they 'should make a statement defining...'. Does this mean that they ought to, but do not have to? 'Make a statement' adds nothing to the sense.
4. and then after...' Does this means that users could start by determining the number of required state variables? Are they being given the second stage, or not?
5. 'has been determined'. Users were told that they 'should define...'. Now some unidentified person is going to 'determine'. Is this a separate function of somebody else? The passive is always unhelpful in instructions, as it leaves too many questions unanswered (see also pp. 92–4).

6. 'chosen': another passive verb. Who chose, and when? Are 'determined' and 'chosen' two stages or one?
7. 'you can determine', well, yes, but should they? Must they?
8. 'you': who is 'you'?
9. 'both': there are two sets of functions to be determined. Both at once?
10. 'and', three times. How should this section be divided?

Instructions: suggested version

Design of a state machine
1. Define the state machine in terms of a state diagram.
2. Determine the number of state variables required.
3. Choose state representations.
4. Determine the next-state functions of the present state and inputs.
5. Determine the output functions of the present state and inputs.

▶ Chapter 5

5.1 Levels of formality

This is a test not only of appropriate levels of formality, but also of tact! We have mentioned 'courtesy', and when an aspect of the work has clearly been mishandled, the documentation has to be clear without accusing anybody.

However, there are many problems with the writing itself:

1. 'done' is an ugly word, and better avoided
2. 'at the end of the day' is a popular cliché, also to be avoided
3. 'start again from scratch' is slang
4. 'it's a pity they didn't bother' is impolite and far too personal in tone
5. the sentence beginning 'Documentation was...' is pompous in tone and unnecessarily wordy
6. Direct questions should usually be avoided in technical writing
7. 'aforementioned' is pompous and unnecessary
8. 'initial' and 'at the beginning' say the same thing.

The members of the team have so far completed three experiments, but the results seem likely to prove inconclusive and the work may have to be repeated. Wider consultation initially and a feasibility study might have highlighted a need for further preliminary work.

5.2 Active and passive

Jim was responsible for the correct running and maintenance of the machine. When it failed to function correctly, his manager investigated, and found that Jim had not only failed to carry out regular maintenance, but had completed the records as if he had done all that was required. The manager saw that the machine was functioning at well below capacity, and that as Jim had not positioned the guard correctly, the operative was at risk. A colleague reported that Jim had been ill at the time.

In the passive version, Jim's responsibilities are much less clear. Should Jim himself have carried out the maintenance, or was somebody else involved? Did Jim falsify the records? Should he have carried out the positioning of the guard? Even the final comment, about Jim's illness, sounds slightly suspicious, as if someone was covering up for Jim's inefficiency.

The active version removes these doubts. Jim had failed to carry out the maintenance, and, what was worse, had actually falsified the records himself. He should have positioned the guard correctly, but had failed to do so. There is no question that Jim is the person to blame at every stage. However, the final sentence sounds a little less like an excuse and so Jim might after all get a bit of sympathy!

This is perhaps an unusually strong case of the passive leaving the actions and the person responsible unclear and the active leaving no doubt, but it is worth remembering that this is generally the difference in impact: if we want to stress the person responsible, we will use the active; if we don't, we will use the passive.

5.3 Linking words and phrases

Interestingly, this passage has not been written by a professional or even an experienced writer but by a student with a feeling for the flow of the language. This level of clear, fluent writing can be achieved by most engineers who want to produce a good style for everyday use.

Structures which are most at risk from progressive failure are those that are highly optimised and operate at a high proportion of their ultimate load. Aerospace structures are perhaps the most obvious example of such structures and it is in the design of airframes that much attention has been paid to ensuring fail-safety. Since such structures must have as low a weight as possible, they are optimised to ensure that no part is larger than necessary. However, this means that a variation from the assumed load pattern, as would happen if local damage were sustained, could have a serious effect on members close to the site of damage if allowance is not made for this eventuality. Fail-safe or damage-tolerant design is that which will remain serviceable even after having been damaged. The main method by which this is achieved is the incorporation of alternative load paths into the structure by means of multiple redundancy. Thus, when damage occurs, there are a number of other members which can carry the extra load.

5.4 Persuasive writing
1. The great advantage of shift work is that you will have the opportunity to work in a small, dedicated group. Moreover, variety in your work is promised, and your relative isolation from decision makers and other sources of help means that you get more individual responsibility. Extra money and holiday time more than compensate for any disruption of normal family and social life and possible long-term health problems.

2. Long-term health problems are, it has been suggested, associated with shift work. You may be isolated from the decision makers at work in spite of being in a small, dedicated team, and any variety and individual responsibility you may gain could be undermined by the problem of getting help if you need it. Even more alarming is the difficulty of achieving normal family and social life, whatever the inducements of possible extra money and holiday time.

▶ Chapter 7

7.1 Checking
In the version below, the deliberate mistakes have been highlighted.

Most industrial sheds in the ***area*** are strategically placed on the industrial estate well away ***from [once only]*** the town and towards the motorway. From the mid-1980s, further ***development*** also took place on the old railway sidings. The single-*storey* units are usually large and open-plan. Styles vary *from* brick units with large shutters and few windows to large *corrugated* or *plain* metal units with a skeletal frame and *no windows*. Maintenance is *low*, as is rent. Refurbishment is easy, and *many* units incorporate a mezzanine level. The local area is wide and flat and allows for easy *parking* and good delivery facilities.

Further reading

Kirkman, John, *Good Style: Writing for Science and Technology*, Spon, 1992

Peck, John and Coyle, Martin, *The Student's Guide to Writing*, Palgrave Macmillan 1999

van Emden, Joan, *Effective Communication for Science and Technology*, Palgrave Macmillan, 2001

van Emden, Joan and Becker, Lucinda, *Presentation Skills for Students*, Palgrave Macmillan, 2004

Words and phrases discussed in the text

Index